BETWEEN TWO SOULS

Donna MacLeod

authorHOUSE®

AuthorHouse™
1663 Liberty Drive, Suite 200
Bloomington, IN 47403
www.authorhouse.com
Phone: 1-800-839-8640

This book is a work of non-fiction. Unless otherwise noted, the author
and the publisher make no explicit guarantees as to the accuracy of
the information contained in this book and in some cases, names of
people and places have been altered to protect their privacy.

First published by AuthorHouse   9/25/2009

ISBN: 978-1-4490-2891-6 (sc)

Library of Congress Control Number: 2009909544

Printed in the United States of America
Bloomington, Indiana

This book is printed on acid-free paper.

PART I

Chapter 1

Trembling in fear, she ran toward the door in a state of blank mindlessness, her eyes blazing wildly and a burning sensation sweeping upward from her feet. The burning scorched her eyes, causing her head to ache. She began to choke while clearing an acrid taste that had developed in her mouth, then slapped open the door loud and angry. She looked to her left, where a beautiful red cardinal perched on the forsythia bush near the driveway. Her eyes widened in confusion. The cardinal looked back but did not move. For a moment, their eyes were locked.

Dressed in one of her many floral housecoats, she was slight in stature. Set into her full, round face, her emerald eyes were glazed over and unfocused. Her tiny mouth was struggling to form words as her mind raced trying to process what was happening but could not. Barely conscious of her actions, she looked up the hill. With a sweep of her loose golden hair, she began to rotate her head, and while moving her head furiously, she ran, still puffing short gasps of breath. Then her mouth opened wide.

Long and high pitched, the primal terror scream was heard at the far end of the street. As neighbors ran furiously from their homes to see what the clamor was, some thought for a moment that it was all a ruse, part of the day. It was Halloween 1989.

Frances, the first neighbor to arrive, had heard the scream as she was baking biscotti in her kitchen. She stopped rolling her dough just long enough to determine that the sound was a human scream, not some animals fighting on the street. She ran toward the noise, and stood face to face with Connie, who was motioning incoherently toward the house. Without asking any questions, Frances reached the door, which was still slightly ajar. Connie stumbled in behind her. The house was silent. Frances stood in the living room for a moment, and Connie came up from behind. With anguish distorting her face, Connie staggered toward the bedroom, and summoned another scream. Frances looked into the bedroom just long enough to observe the horror. She ran into Connie's kitchen, grabbed the telephone, and dialed 911. Connie stood in the doorway trembling, her eyes fixated on the scene before her. Frances returned and held onto her so she would not fall. A tense silence prevailed as they stood embraced searching for any sign of life from his body. Still not able to speak, Connie fell to her knees shaking by the bedside. Then they heard the ambulance coming down the street. With its siren blaring, it lurched to a stop in front of the home, where a small cluster of neighbors had now gathered. Three paramedics sprang out and began unloading from the back of the truck. Frances met them at the door.

"He's in there," she said, pointing. "He's not breathing."

"Thank you, ma'am. We'll take it from her," the paramedic replied.

Another paramedic pulled out a stretcher and some other equipment, and they hurried into the house.

He was being moved onto the floor. From somewhere outside his body, somewhere near the ceiling, he watched them lay him on the rose colored shag carpet that was secured to the living room floor. He heard noises. He wasn't sure if they were coming from him. His eyes flapped open, huge and gaping, at two strangers in nameless horror. When trying to revive him with chest compressions failed, the paramedics began using an external defibrillator. Again, they followed with another ten minutes of compressions, until they finally were able to detect a faint pulse and some shallow breathing. They placed a line in the patient's arm. He closed his eyes. His skin was pale and sheened with sweat. He felt his body shake as it was being prodded. Then he was being lifted. Again. The paramedics packed up their equipment, draped a blanket over him, and transported to the nearest medical facility, which was only five minutes away, leaving his sixty-five-year-old mother sitting slumped in a living room chair—paralyzed.

A peculiar uneasiness blanketed me from the moment I woke. Looking around the room, my eyes widened. I shrugged and readied myself for the task at hand. Usually, the anticipation of the day lifted my spirits, as I remembered Halloween through the eyes of a child. I thought of Mom, reveling in the festivities as each year she would host another party for me and my friends in our damp, dark turn-of-the-century basement. With an uneven dirt floor, one tiny, nearly opaque window, and cobwebs clinging lazily from almost every hand hewn beam, the basement provided the perfect setting for screams, treats, and dancing.

"Great party, Donna. Great food. What fun!

"Yes," I reply. "Lots of fun." Then without warning, the lights were turned down low. The clamor hushed, and all eyes turned toward the staircase. Standing huddled in place with our arms wrapped tightly around each other, our eyes search widely for reaction. We don't dare speak for fear of interrupting the pervasive silence that has swept us up in its path. But soon a loud thumping breaks the conqueror's hold, and the basement stairs seem to echo with each and every thump. There is a pause after the last thump, and with that pause we expel such blood-curdling shrieks that they should have been enough to send the creature back to where it came from, but they didn't. There before us is a monster wearing blue jeans and sneakers. The mask seems to open at an unnatural orifice, and it howls so realistically that you swear a wolf is skinning the hide right off your back.

My brother Phil always the prankster, wearing the scariest, most gruesome masks he could find at the local costume store each year. Mom follows behind laughing hysterically and carrying yet another bowl of cupcakes, candy, and soda. Even in her golden years, when most of her neighbors had turned out their front lights and stopped giving out candy, Mom was ready at the front door with bowls brimming, a smile on her face and a witch's hat on her head.

Many years had passed. I now had two girls of my own and tried to carry on the traditions Mom held so dear. I smiled at the memories, shuffled on my slippers, and wrapped up in my bathrobe. I walked down the front staircase and opened the door. The sky was gray and dull. It was unseasonably warm, the air thick with anticipation of rain and an innocuous veil hanging over the town. I felt a gentle breeze churn silently over my head. I paused and closed the door. Hmm, I thought, it must be the weather.

Within seconds, my girls were stumbling down the stairs behind me, almost tripping over their costumes. They settled in at the breakfast table and began shoveling cereal into their anxious little mouths.

Nicole, at nine years old, was dressed as a geisha. The ebony wig styled into an enormous pouf, black liner for eyebrows, porcelain skin, and fire engine red lipstick were sensational, and a complete contrast to her own blonde hair, green eyes, and peaches-and-cream skin. She wore a lovely authentic kimono, brought back from a recent trip to Japan. Nicole was every bit a little lady; demure and sweet, she loved to wear dresses.

"Look at you two. You look great!" I said. "Too bad Nana won't get to see you all dressed up. You know how she loves Halloween."

"It's okay, Mom. Maybe you can drive us over to see her after we come home from trick-or-treating," Nicole replied.

"I don't think so, honey. It will be very late, but we'll see how the evening goes."

I grabbed their sweaters and gestured toward the door.

"We have to move quicker if we're going to make the bus. Kimmy, grab your juice box. Nicole, don't forget your wig. You both are dawdling like zombies. Should I have dressed you both like zombies?"

"No, Mom. Girls aren't zombies. Boys are," Nicole insisted.

"Oh really. Fine then. Out the door with both of you."

We reached the bus stop, where parents had already staked out prime locations for the photo shoot. The children were waving at their parents, who were busy flashing away, and as was customary, most of the girls were princesses, while the boys were monsters of some sort. By the street corner, some of the boys were deliberately intimidating the girls, the girls fluttering off with their crowns and halos hugging their heads and shoulders for protection. Finally, the bus arrived, and Nicole boarded.

"I want to go too Mommy!" Kimmy wailed.

"I will bring you to school later on today. You must wait."

"No."

"Yes." Stubborn child, I thought.

My younger daughter, Kimberly, at almost three, was a true tomboy. She hated dresses, preferring jeans, and handled every slimy creature native to the planet. Trees were a favorite too—she attempted to climb them with the best of the boys. Kimmy has auburn eyes and dark brown hair. Even as a child, she possessed that untamed look. She was dressed as a ferocious lion, complete with the roar. Very independent, Kimmy had a mind of her own.

We arrived at the party at 1:30. When I opened the door to the school, laughter hit me first, followed by cookie and cupcake crumbs strewn through the hallways like little lost tokens left behind by Hansel and Gretel. When we entered the classroom, we noticed children with face paint oozing in transparent, vivid patches down their animated faces. Homeroom moms had prepared a variety of treats, and the children were gorging themselves.

As the party was winding down, I packed up my girls' belongings and we exited the building together. Ahead of me, they were skipping. Their legs couldn't keep up with their excitement. While walking toward the car, iciness raked my flesh. I paused for a moment and looked up. *From a passing cloud*, I thought, then opened the car door.

Arriving home shortly thereafter, I settled the girls in for a snack and began walking up to the attic for their candy baskets.

While walking back down the stairs, the telephone rang, but before I could answer it I froze in place. I felt the hair rising on my forearm. My jaw clenched. That earlier uneasiness gripped me again, and I tried not to convey this emotion to my girls. Finally reaching the kitchen, I caught the phone on the last ring.

"Hello, I heard through the receiver.

"Hello," I said, my stomach beginning to pitch.

"This is Uncle Sam. Philip was just taken to the hospital in an ambulance. You must get there immediately."

His message was non-specific. I wondered why. Guarded, I had waited all day for the bomb to drop. Now it had.

"I'm on my way."

Running around in confusion, I began to gather the items Nicole and Kim would need that evening.

"What are you doing, Mom?" Nicole asked.

"Listen, honey. That call was from Uncle Sam. Uncle Philip has been rushed to the hospital, and I need to get there as fast as I can."

"But it's Halloween."

"I know. Please be a big girl and look after Kimmy for me. I am calling Mrs. Landers. She will take care of you until Dad or I get home."

Kimmy grabbed my leg and began to wail, and Nicole's eyes filled as well.

"Please don't cry," I said as I lifted the receiver and called my neighbor, Sheila, to explain the situation, or what little I knew of it.

"Don't worry about it," she said. "They will be fine with us. I will call Mark for you. Take your time, and good luck."

I dropped the girls off and began my drive north to the city hospital. Usually bustling with traffic, the road seemed paved for me. My mind was as erratic as my driving, and my expectations were unclear. My breathing was coming in shallow gasps, as I arrived at the hospital fifteen minutes earlier than logistically possible. I parked my car in a handicap parking the space—the only one available—and ran full speed into the emergency room, adrenaline pumping fast into every vein in my body. After identifying myself to a nurse, I was admitted and led through the corridors, where my eyes fixed on a staggering sight.

I cannot even begin to describe the sheer terror in his eyes as he gazed up at mine. Lying silent on a gurney, my brother seemed so tiny and frail in the bed. His small frame was covered with a thin, white blanket. I pulled the blanket up closer to his chin and bent down to kiss his cheek. His face too had become small, pulled painfully tight and thin like a girdle on a fat lady. Attached to a ventilator, Philip was the only patient in this room, which was cold, sterile, and awash in bright light. As a machine roared beside him, he didn't seem to respond. He closed his eyes, which appeared to be too heavy to remain open. My parents flanked him on each side of the bed. My mother was ashen, shaking, and clearly beyond the ability to console. Her head was bent forward toward my brother, a soft whimper emanating from her mouth. On the other side, my father moved slightly so that I could get closer. I bent down, stroked Philip's hand lightly, and whispered, "I'm here. Listen to me. You must fight. Please," I cried.

I repeated these words again and again. Then his eyes began to flutter, and he opened them, looking around confused, as if his vision was blurred. Startled, my body shook for a moment. Clearly, Philip knew I was there; he seemed fully aware of his surroundings, and I sensed he wanted to tell me something by the way he is looking at me, but he couldn't. The breathing tube was set deeply down his throat. I continued my words of encouragement.

He stared at me for a moment longer, his mouth trying to open as if to say something. Instead, he shook his head slightly to one side. There was a haunting sadness in his eyes, that same sadness that had been in his eyes for a very long time. He had struggled to survive these last five years, and I wondered if he was trying to say, *Let me go*, or was he pleading for me to save him. Involuntarily, I reached out, as though my touch might heal him. I rested my hand on his left shoulder in silence, groping for the right words. His eyes were riveted on me.

"Please, you're strong. We need you." I choked and had to catch my breath. "We love you, and this is not your time."

"Ssh now," my father murmured. "Try to stay calm."

My father. Always stoic. How could he be calm now?

I looked down again at Philip. Those piercing emerald eyes were still gazing up at me, his head moving to the side again. Confused, I didn't dare take my eyes off him. I was searching for a sign, any sign, that would clarify his wishes. A moment later, from behind the privacy curtain, a doctor and a nurse appeared. The doctor moved toward us, then introduced himself. He approached Mom first.

"Mrs. Tullio, I am Dr. Kane.

Dr. Kane was heavyset, about forty, with a mop of black hair flopping on his forehead.   "Can you tell me exactly how everything unfolded today?"

Mom began to speak but soon paused, looked at Philip, and began crying again. Dr. Kane grabbed her elbow gently.

"Why don't we talk out in the hallway," Dr. Kane said, gesturing us toward the door.

My parents and I walked out slowly, each of us turning back every few steps and gorging our minds with Philip's presence. I could still see the image of his eyes in his face staring at me with abject fear. I didn't have a clue what he was trying to say as he gaped at me. I closed the door behind me. Out in the hallway, Dad delivered the story, as Mom was far too upset to think or speak with any real clarity. I listened in horror.

"Philip was having lunch with my wife in our home, where we cared for him. He had just returned from a trip to the bank. As they were eating, he began to complain about excruciating pains in his legs. He was pale and told my wife that he was nauseous. He said he was going to the bedroom to lie down, and that he felt horrible. When my wife asked what was wrong, he said that he had never felt this way before. She told him she would get his blood testing monitor to check his glucose levels. She heard him walking very slowly down the corridor to the bedroom. She couldn't have been gone for much more than a minute when she heard an unsettling noise. She dropped her supplies and ran toward the bedroom. When she reached the room, she found him, on his back, arms and legs outstretched, his eyes fixed on the ceiling."

Oh my God, I thought. Her firstborn child lay there dead, right in front of her eyes. He was only forty-two. I shook at the thought, and my chill returned. I looked over at Dad. He had delivered the story with extraordinary clarity.

"Okay," Dr. Kane said. "Can someone give me his medical history?"

"Yes, I can."

"And you are?" the doctor asked.

"Philip's sister."

"Okay."

"His medical history is complex, but I'll try to simplify it and bring you up to date. Philip has been a diabetic since he was seventeen. When he was thirty-seven, his kidneys began to fail. That was five years ago. My father donated a kidney to him, but he rejected it within three years. He is currently back on dialysis." I paused.

"The diagnosis is fairly obvious," said Dr. Kane. "He has had cardiac arrest due to the complications of his renal failure and the ravaging of his heart from the hemodialysis. Our main concern is that he was without a heartbeat for an extended period of time, at least fifteen minutes, I am told by the paramedics. More than likely, he has suffered some residual brain damage as a result of oxygen deprivation."

My mouth opened, but nothing came out.

"You may need to make a choice here," he said reluctantly.

I listened respectfully, absorbing all the information, hoping I would never be called upon to make use of it. This was a judgment I would not want to take responsibility for, but I knew my parents would look to me for guidance. They always had. My father was such a brilliant man, but never wanted to make the really tough choices in life. He left that to Mom, and now me. I never understood his reluctance to take a stand. Why me, I thought. Always me. How could I make a decision that would alter all our lives forever?

The meaning of life seemed to diminish on the waves of the steady stares that waited, half full of doubt, half full of hope, for a miracle to be performed. I felt Mom's eyes on me, pleading for help. I diverted my eyes from hers for a moment. When I looked up again, Dad had glanced over at me, trying to read my face. He opened his mouth for a moment to speak, but his lips quivered, soundless. His face wrinkled up in confusion, and he shook his head slowly. He shook it again and again. Still, no words. At this point, Mom was leaning against Dad and the wall, hoping one would provide her enough support to prevent collapse. I could barely see her face—she never lifted it—but I could see the constant stream of tears flowing down her cheeks into her mouth. I shook myself back to the present and thought about this dilemma over and over again, not coming to any sound conclusion. I couldn't possibly say good-bye knowing that I was responsible for making that ultimate and seemingly unnatural decision to end his life. No one spoke for several more minutes. I think we were all in shock at this point, even Dad. Every head turned and questioning eyes stared at me.

Dr. Kane broke the numbing silence. "I will need a list of his medications. Can someone get that for me immediately?"

"I'll go get his medications," Dad said. "We live only a few minutes up the road. I'll be back quickly."

"I'll go with you," Mom said. "I don't want you to travel alone. Will you be all right?" Mom asked me.

"Yes, you go. I'll be here if anyone needs me. Drive carefully."

Mom linked her arm through Dad's as they ambled out of the hospital. I suppose they needed to stay together at this crucial moment to take some comfort in each other, although Dad was never a comforter. Meanwhile, I sat all alone in the waiting room and attempted to collect my thoughts as my heart pounded through my chest. I could not think, my mind felt like an enormous vacuum, sucking me away, making me feel faint. Just when I thought my head was about to fall forward, I was jolted by a loudspeaker.

"Code blue, code blue, ER," the speaker blared. I sat straight up now, straining to hear any indication of the situation. I could hear footsteps scampering quickly past my room and into the room across the hall, where my brother lay. Again, the speaker blared, and there were more footsteps. I tried to stand and open the door in hopes of seeing something telling, but I couldn't will my legs to move. Fearing I would fall, I simply sat without movement. I sat and I sat. Ultimately, directly behind my door, I heard a conversation going on in hushed tones. There were more footsteps, and I gave a nervous start as Dr. Kane and a nurse appeared through the door. They closed the door slowly and walked over to me. The nurse followed slowly behind Dr. Kane, a slight smile on her face. Or was it a smile? I questioned as I looked at her. I couldn't tell. On the other hand, Dr. Kane seemed solemn and contrite. I felt the need to gulp but could not, even my mouth was frozen. I fought to breathe, my heart hammering. The nurse took a step in front of the doctor, walked over, and knelt beside me. She laid her hand on my hand. Then Dr. Kane said, "We tried. I'm sorry. He is gone."

I did not respond, nor did I ask any questions, just stared at them without words. I could not move or speak. I felt as though I had been hit by an asteroid. I began to cry quietly, and still disoriented, my upper body seemed to sway. *This is not happening*, I thought. My inner self was echoing, as I felt like I was spinning or being pulled inside out. As I lifted my sagging head, the nurse said, "I can take you to see him if you would like."

"No. I just need to sit alone for a minute."

"I'll be right at the nurses' station if you need me, dear."

"Thank you," I replied.

I felt powerless; the unthinkable had happened.

Dr. Kane and the nurse left the room with hardly a sound. I tried to straighten my body, but it was immobile, yet my heart was racing through my chest. Through my tears, I began to construct a visual biography. Images flowed into each other from what seemed like another time. Sledding, igloos, bike rides. My fondest childhood memories included my brother sharing, laughing, caring about me. He never thought me a nuisance. The imagery continued, as I brought back to life faces I hadn't seen in decades and felt my heart quicken as another memory came back to me.

The door opened, and my parents, unaware of what had happened, stood before me. My mother stopped, her mouth dropping open. I saw horror in her face. Dad took one look at my condition and stood frozen in horrified revelation. I tried to rise from my chair but couldn't, and without a spoken word, they knew. My mother looked at me. I had never seen eyes so bleak. I saw her body stiffen, and there was a cry of desperation. My mother doubled over, collapsing across the knees with a heavy sob. Dad tried to catch her, but she was too quick for his aging reflexes.

"Oh God," she wailed. "Why, oh God."

Wracked with sobs, she fell to the floor. It wasn't a slow fall. Her lower body lurched forward with a sudden thud, face first. I knew at this moment that this would be the beginning of the end for my mother.

Halloween 1989, the day the world came to an abrupt stop.

CHAPTER 2

Mom couldn't recall one second of the dark tornado that had swept her up in those first few weeks that followed. She had been medicated heavily throughout the ordeal and had no recollection of the funeral. This added another layer of suffering that we could not control, as she had been deprived of her last moments with her son. We had no choice. Dad and I made the decision along with the doctors. Without the medication, she would not have been able to attend the services. Dad tried to hold us all together. He seemed to do this quite well, not ever breaking down.

November arrived with its cold, cutting rain. It was another early morning for Dad. He rose at 6:30 and prepared the breakfast he had for over forty years: a soft-boiled egg, toast, cereal, juice, and tea. He took his morning shower, washed his breakfast dishes, and put them in the drainer to dry. The house was still fragrant from all the flowers and plants people had sent. Dad's nostrils dilated wide like a breathless mare. While sweet and fragrant, the house smelled like "death." The word made him gulp hard. After he dressed, he went into the bedroom and kissed Mom good-bye. He tried to be tender, but it wasn't in his nature, and he was too old to change.

"I'm leaving now," he said. "Are you gonna be all right?"

A faint mumble came from the bed. He hoped that meant yes.

"Call Donna if you need anything, okay?"

No response.

Dad turned, closed the door, and walked out, leaving Mom to deal with the death inside.

Dad had returned to work one week after Philip's funeral. He thought this would be a distraction for him, but he found his motions were robotic, and he had difficulty clearing his thoughts. Always the point man, he rarely delegated authority. He liked to be in control, but his focus was skewed, his concentration coming in small spurts. His closest friends worked with him at the printing company. At lunch they avoided speaking of the tragedy, trying to clear Frank's mind by playing cards. At the end of this particular game his closest friend Lenny asked, "Frankie, how's Connie doing?"

"Not good," he said, shaking his head aimlessly. "She's not eating or sleeping. I give her pills in the morning and when I come home from work. I don't dare leave them there for fear that she may take the entire bottle. She cries most of the day."

"God, Frankie. I'm so sorry. I've known Connie most of my life. This must be killing her."

"It is. It's an awful thing. The doctor has recommended she see a psychiatrist, but Donna and I agree that she just needs time to grieve."

"Well, take it one day at a time, Frankie."

"Yes, that's what we're trying to do."

Dad left work early that day to visit the cemetery. As he drove up to the lot, he felt a heaviness in his chest, and his hands tingled on the steering wheel. He waited a moment until the feeling came back, then got out of the car and shuffled slowly up the small hill. He stood for some time, perhaps thirty minutes—he wasn't sure. The freshly turned earth was as raw as his emotions.

As time stood still, an unfamiliar sensation swept over him. While very present on this exact spot, a remoteness seemed to grip his body. He tried to move but was immobile. A damp, stale odor wafted past, and Dad's head and eyes began to feel heavy and fixated on the landscape, which was slowly beginning to bleed color. First, the grass turned an ethereal white, then the sky began its bleed from blue to gray. Dad squinted forward at the gravestone, which oddly seemed aged with centuries-old patina and no longer resembled Philip's gravestone. He was drawn toward it; it now seemed smaller than the rest. He tried to read the name as his vision was blurred by the impenetrable mist around him. Joseph. Novia. Joseph Novia. Where had he heard this name, and where had Philip's gravestone gone? He turned his head to find it. Some of the gravestones were tilting slightly forward, ready to collapse. He blinked and found his eyes probing the cherub figures in the waterless fountains, then twitched with a vibration that sent a current through his body. Suddenly, he was aware of a burst of energy, all directed beneath his feet. What was that banging? Dad looked down. The rectangular image was darker and looser than the surrounding dirt. Just weeks before, he had buried his son on this exact spot.

"What the hell is that?" he asked out loud.

It sounded like something banging steel. Something or someone. He looked around him. There seemed to be silence everywhere, except beneath his feet. *He's trying to get out!* he thought, and he dropped to his knees. He began scooping the dirt up in his bare hands. Faster and faster until he could get to the vault, open it and save his son.

A low, gray sky threatened rain. My anguish on this frigid November day was so overwhelming I felt compelled to visit my brother's grave. I had visited often since his death, and I wished I could just see him one more time. Another hug, but that would never be. At times I would say the most outrageous things to Mark.

"Do you think I could see him one more time? Could someone do that for me?"

"Donna, you need to get a grip on yourself," he replied with my twisted face in his warm hands. I had been the calm one, the person who organized the entire funeral, the person in charge, but my strong exterior was an illusion. My insides were incensed.

I pulled into the cemetery. The place, once foreign, was now a refuge. I turned a corner and drove slowly toward the gravesite. As I continued to drive, I could see a car in the distance, and a person on the ground. On approach, I realized it was my dad. "Oh my God!" I shouted. I thought he had collapsed, until I noticed he was in a kneeling position, his bare hands moving furiously in front of him. I jumped out of the car and ran toward him. He didn't even flinch at the noise I had created, but continued on with his quest.

"Dad, what on earth are you doing? God, I thought I would come up here to sit for a few minutes, and I see you digging."

Dad's eyes were crazed, moving wildly in unison with his hands. His white shirt had become soiled, as had his face and hair. With ferocious digging, the air around him swirled thick with dirt, billowing high above. I could see the muscles protrude in his forearms.

"There was a banging right under this exact spot!"

As he continued to dig furiously, he realized that the landscape was once again becoming vibrant with color. He turned his head from side to side, noticing the greenness of the grass and the blueness of the sky. His eyes opened wider. He began to feel his arms moving, his eyelids flapping while trying to keep the sweat from entering. The banging was diminishing, becoming more of a light tapping.

"Dad, please stop. This is crazy!"

"Crazy, is it? Then you explain it!"

"I can't, but I don't hear anything. I'm taking you home."

"No," he said, continuing to dig. "I tell you I heard a banging, right here." He pointed to the small hole he had begun to dig.

"Dad, stop it now," I demanded.

"I need to get to your brother! I tell you he was banging!"

I waited. He ignored me and continued to dig, but I could see that his arms were tiring. "Dad, please," I pleaded again.

I gripped his shoulders tightly from behind. He looked up at me, the wildness in his eyes beginning to diminish. His ebony eyes were now narrowed, I saw my father's anguish there for the first time. With a final sigh, his hands stopped, and his muscles loosened. Exhaling, he dropped his shoulders, a clear sign of surrender, then turned to face me.

"Fine, you can follow me home if you want, but don't breathe a word of this to your mother. Not a word."

"Of course not."

I walked Dad into the house and checked on Mom, who appeared to be sleeping, then called Mark.

"You need to meet me up the cemetery. Can you come now?"

"What's wrong?" he asked.

"I'm not sure, but meet me up there in fifteen minutes."

"Okay."

Mark and I arrived at almost the same time and walked up to the tombstone. It was quiet. We used our bare hands to try to scoop the lifted dirt back into the small hole Dad had dug.

"I don't understand it. He just kept repeating it over and over."

"Maybe it was just some delirious rambling," Mark said.

"Dad, delirious, never."

"Well, I can't find an explanation. Can you?" he asked.

I came up blank. *Crazy, is it?* I thought. Dad was the most grounded person I knew. If he said he heard something, I would be inclined to think he had. But what could it have possibly been? What on this earth?

*****

Mom remained in an agitated state for many months. Indeed, she grew worse and was taken over by one malady after another. Soon the symptoms manifested themselves into actual physiological conditions, and her deterioration began. There were entire days when she could not speak and had to be held up in a half-sitting position just to take a sip of tea. Unable to sleep at night, she became subject to the most excruciating dreams, and even with medicines to remedy her, they were unleashed.

In one drug-induced dream that followed, Philip was trying to bang his way out of his casket, unable to get above the ground. Mom watched in horror as he struggled, fear blazing in his eyes. When she finally woke, shaking, she was looking up into Dad's face.

"I just had the most awful dream," she cried. "Philip was banging trying to get out of his casket, but he couldn't. The banging, the banging," she shrieked.

Dad's heart skipped a beat. *How could this be?* he thought. It was just too coincidental. How could she have had a dream that so perfectly depicted his scene at the cemetery? He held Mom to his chest, his arms trying to control her shaking. His mind churned with confusion, as he tightened his grip. Finally, she passed from shaking to shivering; then, too weary to continue, she sat still. He didn't know what to say, and was incapable of comforting her in this state. Yes, he loved her, but he wasn't a sentimental man. If he aspired to any mastery, it was to the rules of science, not emotion. But how did the rules of science apply to his experience in the cemetery? he wondered.

CHAPTER 3

Standing in the center of Haymarket Square, the nondescript open-air produce market on Blackstone Street in Boston's West End. Frank Tullio thought the sun had never felt so hot. The flies were swarming around his pushcart, trying to scavenge the ripe lemons. Lifting his head, he blinked, trying not to think about the home he would be returning to at the end of the day.

It is 1928, and Frank is eight years old. Scrawny and dirty, he is the fourth of eleven children born to Maria and Philippe Tullio, immigrants from Sicily. Poverty was an element of his life before he gasped for his first breath. Philippe's sons were bred to support the family, and they did, almost from the time they were weaned. Philippe, an unskilled worker, found assimilating into life in America challenging.

This struggle created strong bonds among people, as families lived in the same house, and in very close quarters. The concrete buildings were a sharing pool where clotheslines hung from the tenements, running across in parallel formation from window to window. Frank and his siblings played on the stone pavement below, running around in circles heedlessly beneath the flapping clothes. There seemed to be a love of life, of family, of their new country, and a strong sense of hope, but some children grew up with hearts as hungry as their bellies, feeling that one day they would run out of everything again.

On this day, the square was bustling. Pushcarts brimming with fruits and vegetables were lined up in uneven rows. There was a rampant shuffling of feet. The shrill of loud voices, like crows squawking at each other, repeated their duets, trying to shout out the others and draw the customers to their cart.

"Five lemons for five cents, five lemons for five cents," small Frank attempted to bellow. He stood by his pushcart eyeing the apples in the cart next to his. He would much rather be selling apples. Apples were tasty and sweet. Lemons were not. They made him feel sick. He thought about snatching an apple for himself now and then to quench the dire hunger burning in his gut.

"What are you looking at kid?" his older brother Nicky asked.

"Nothing," said Frank.

"Keep your eyes on your own cart."

"Yeah, Nicky, I heard ya."

The haggling continues.

The day passed slowly. Well dressed people with their perfectly dressed children purchased lemons from Frank. He noticed the children in their fine clothes and looked down at his own rags. His shoes were without laces and had holes on the soles. His T-shirt and pants were hand-me-downs, tattered from years of laundering. His black hair was dirty, as were his arms, legs, and face. He did not look like these children. Even at eight years of age, Frank understood his status in life. That evening, while sitting at the dinner table with far too little food, little Frank concocted his first scheme.

"Apples, apples, nice red apples," the old man shouted. "Five for ten cents."

The old man had his eyes set squarely on Frank, who he had noticed was edging closer and closer to his pushcart. Nick had set out to the pier to buy more lemons, and Frank was in charge of the cart. The apple cart was only five feet away, but Frank's arms were not long enough to reach. He knew he had to create a diversion so that the old man would never see the pillage. Frank's throat was parched, the aching in his belly playing a symphony. Now was the time, he concluded. Frank grabbed a lemon, tossed it up into the air and over the old man's head. When the old man looked up, Frank snatched two apples. Suddenly, the old man turned toward Frank, his eyebrows raised at the corners. He looked angry, then began to count his apples. Frank could hardly breathe while the old man counted. He prayed Nick would hurry back. The old man had the last apple in his hand when he shouted, "Thief!"

Frank abandoned his pushcart full of lemons and ran, with the old man in pursuit. He stumbled over an obstacle and flung his arms out with a startled cry. As his feet fell out from under him, he rolled untidily down until he hit a stack of large boxes next to the Jordan Marsh Department Store. Scrambling to his feet, he looked behind him. He had lost the old man.

He breathed a huge sigh of relief and entered the store, his mind racing. Frank knew that if the police had seen the altercation and taken chase, he would be in big trouble. One of his brothers had already had run-ins with the law, and the family was trying to avoid drawing any more attention to themselves. The police were predominantly Irish and had now ascended to the ruling class in the city. With great satisfaction, they would round up the young Italian boys, delivering them on cue to a judge. The Italian parents, most whom could not speak English, would not fight the charges, and the city would generate money. Fearing deportation, the immigrants in the West End rarely ventured off their own blocks. Some even stopped speaking Italian except in their own homes, and they encouraged their children to become Americanized.

Still running, Frank saw a moving stairway up ahead. Without caution, he sprinted and caught the handrail beneath the rubber.

The pain sent Frank spiraling. He dared not look at his hand, but he felt something warm oozing down his fingers. Then, everything began to whiten. The next time he looked up, it was into the eyes of two strangers—a doctor and a nurse, he gathered from their attire. Frank was dizzy and looked around the room trying to get his bearings. The walls were closing in on either side, and the ceiling was dropping. The air smelled dank. The doctor looked grim, Frank thought, and everyone was speaking in hushed tones. The door opened at that point, and Frank caught sight of the hem of his mother's black skirt, but before she could approach, the doctor gestured her back into the hallway. She followed reluctantly.

"Mrs. Tullio, we must remove your son's hand."

"No speak English," Frank's mother replied.

Doctor Gardner was young and ambitious. He peered through his spectacles at the image before him. Frank's mother still wore the apron bearing small patches of white flour. She smelled of fresh bread. She was a dark, looming woman, not particularly handsome, heavyset and dressed in black. Her hands and lips were moving rapidly.

"Find an interpreter!" he ordered the nurse. "I have no time for this woman!"

The nurse flinched and then moved to carry out his order.

Frank was barely conscious, but he could hear his mother's senseless mumblings next to him. An orderly entered the room and began rolling Frank's bed toward the door.

"Get the operating room ready for this boy, quickly," Dr. Gardner ordered.

Frank's mother was still rambling, her large hands beating her apron. Doctor Gardner grazed her in passing.

Inside the examining room, Frank lay on the gurney nearing the door. Doctor Gardner reappeared. Cold, steel eyes blazed down on him. Frank's breath became thick in his throat.

"Your hand must come off, Frank. Do you understand?"

"No, no, *non la mano*," Frank's mother shouted in Italian.

The orderly began to open the door. Frank was shaking in disbelief. He tried to jump from the gurney, but the orderly strapped him down. Frank saw a bright light from beneath the door. Breaking the restraints, he lunged toward Doctor Gardner, then ran for the door. On the other side was Nick.

Frank lay alone on a bed. This was unusual in a home where there were usually four to a bed, heels touching. It was quiet, and oddity as well. There was no one to coddle him, and this wasn't something he even remotely expected. He sighed, tears in his eyes, and thought about his plan that went terribly wrong. A large white bandage lay on a pillow beside him. Inside was his hand. His whole hand.

Chapter 4

Sneaking peaks from behind Maria's apron, Concetta Sava-ca chased her younger brothers around in circles. The store was not large, and they were confined to the back room for much of the day. Maria seemed annoyed, but Orazio laughed and scooped them all up in his massive arms.

In 1920, four years before Concetta was born, Maria and Orazio had arrived from Sicily. Concetta was the oldest of three children and the only daughter. Her parents owned a fish market. Days were long for the Savacas, but the rewards were many. Orazio was not fluent in English, but he still managed to build a successful business. With a trombone voice and a violin smile, Orazio was admired by many. The Savacas were a hardworking family who believed in equal responsibility and benevolence.

When Concetta was old enough, she cared for her younger brothers at home. Maria and Orazio worked long, hard days, and Concetta contributed her share. After she returned home from school, she spent the remainder of her day chasing the boys around and doing some light cleaning. They lived in a spotlessly clean three-story apartment building on the West End's "upper end," considered the better side of town. Her devotion to her family did not go unnoticed, as her parents lavished beautiful gifts on their daughter. Fine clothing and furs were considered extravagant, but

Orazio shared his money generously with his family. The family indulged in opera and ballroom dancing. Orazio's generosity was spread beyond his own family as well.

His heart was as large as the man himself, and he would frequently give food to the poor. This food could have easily been sold the following day, but there were a vast population of poor people in the West End of Boston in the 1930s and 1940s, and Orazio felt the need to help those less fortunate than him. Frank's family, with Frank in tow, along with dozens of other families, would arrive at Orazio's store once they had run out of food. Concetta and Frank had spent their last years of childhood together during the Depression, but they never knew it.

One afternoon, on a cool December morning in 1942, Josephine Fruzetti called the Savacas' home. Josephine was Concetta's closest friend. She was also the antithesis of Concetta, or Connie as her friends called her. Josephine had sharp features, and dark eyes and hair. She was witty and engaging. Her family struggled, but she never complained. Connie and Josephine had run into each other earlier in the day at Orazio's store and discussed going out for the evening.

There had been a light snow a few days before, just a crust under the trees, and mud everywhere else. It was still quite cold.

"I think we should take the train," Josephine said. "I don't want to be soaked with muddy shoes when we arrive at the dance hall."

"That sounds good," Connie replied.

She had seen Jimmy Dorsey's orchestra live, as well as Glenn Miller's. With tension and deprivation of a country at war, people had been driven to spending lavish amounts of money for entertainment, money they didn't have. They were anxious to be distracted, and live entertainment seemed to be what they embraced.

As the train approached the stop, Connie removed the compact from her purse and touched up her lips and eyes. Her large eyes were vibrant green, almost emerald, like her father's. Like Orazio, they were warm and welcoming, and sometimes intense.

When they arrived at the dance hall, Josephine entered first. As she pulled her friend along, all heads turned. Connie looked ravishing this evening in a teal satin dress with a black sash. The color was a beautiful contrast to her light chestnut hair. Black satin shoes and a small black clutch completed her elegant ensemble. All eyes were on her, and within seconds, all the girls clamored around.

> "Well, another dress added to the collection," Anna mocked.
> "Leave her alone. You're just jealous," Mary scolded. Mary was a childhood friend, someone Connie could trust. As children they had gone to camp together, and shared their innermost thoughts.

"Come with me, Connie. There's someone I want you to meet," Mary said with a glint in her dark brown eyes. Connie didn't reply, but followed Mary with some apprehension. Mary guided Connie through the crowds toward the back of the dance hall, near the exits. There, three guys had congregated. As the girls approached, the guys stood erect. Taking immediate notice, one set of eyes caught Connie's.

"Hi. I'm Frank," he replied. "Mary's brother."

"Oh." Connie seemed startled.

Frank was dashing. With piercing brown eyes and chiseled features, he resembled Tyrone Power. He had full, inviting lips and perfect white teeth. Connie found his smile menacing, and she began to shrink into herself.

"Well, I can see there's no further need for introductions," Mary said as she tugged on the arms of the two other guys, pulling them away from the couple.

Connie was uncomfortable being alone in a corner with Frank. She bowed her head and withdrew her eyes from his mouth.

"So, how do you know my kid sister?"

"Oh, years ago we went to camp together, and I still see her around town occasionally."

"I see."

He inched closer toward her, and she stepped back.

"Why are you standing all the way back here by the doors?" Connie asked.

"Well, I guess I'm a bit paranoid. You know a couple of months ago when the Coconut Grove went up in flames?"

"Yes."

"Well, my buddies and I were supposed to be in there that night. The couple in front of us were the last ones to be allowed in that evening. They never came out."

"Oh my God," said Connie. "You must believe in angels."

"Not really," he said. "So, do you wanna dance?"

"Okay," she replied, barely audible.

They stepped out onto the dance floor, brushing shoulders in passing. Connie felt awkward, as it seemed people were staring at them. Then Frank reached for her hand. She extended it gracefully. He put an arm around her waist and pulled her closer. Connie had been dancing on her father's feet for as long as she could remember. She could dance in her sleep, she was that good. As each song ended, he held onto her and stayed that way until the next song began. He could smell her. He took in her sweet smell, long and deep, and said, "Nice perfume."

"Channel No. 5," she replied.

The crowds watched in envy. Frank never took his eyes off Connie's face, and Connie never looked up at Frank's. Although her feet were weightless, her thoughts were heavy. She wondered if this was the brother Mary had told her about: the one who had one girlfriend after another. He loved them and left them. Her gut told her he was, and his eyes confirmed it.

***

It was hard to see her small body behind the mounds of massive boxes surrounding her. Connie was busy counting new inventory when a voice called out from in front of the glass counter.

"Hi, Connie."

Frank smiled when she looked up. Connie swallowed, a lump in her throat. She wasn't prepared to see him so soon after their first encounter, and she certainly didn't feel presentable in her old dress and apron. Her hair was pulled back and she wore no makeup.

"I'm sorry. I didn't see you walk in," she said as she removed the clasp that held her hair back.

"No problem. I was just walking home from hanging out with the guys, and I thought I'd come by and say hi."

She was about to speak, but before she could, Orazio stepped out in front of her.

"She's working," he said with his burly arms folded in front of him.

"Oh sorry. Maybe later," Frank said as he walked toward the door.

Connie seemed amused when he left, the corners of her mouth lifted. Orazio turned on his heels and flashed a stern look of disapproval.

Frank walked back down the street to the pop shop, where his buddies were anxiously awaiting his return.

"So, did you get a date, a real date this time?" John asked.

"Yeah, I hear it's hard to get past the old man," Sal said.

"How would you know?" asked Frank.

"Are you kidding, Frankie? Don't tell me you haven't heard about the fisherman and his daughter. He has a metal vault around that girl. No one enters without going through the father."

"We'll see about that."

"Frankie, she's a really good girl. Too good for you," said John.

"Thanks, guys. You're real pals. I'll remember that the next time you need me to get you all out of some mess."

Orazio really wasn't a fisherman, but the label seemed to fit his brawny, salty exterior quite well. He spent his early mornings on the docks buying the goods for the store each day, but he never stepped foot on a boat. He didn't like the sea after his experiences coming to America. He was seasick the entire voyage over. Maria nursed him as best she could, but she was fighting an illness as well and was almost turned back when she tried to register at Ellis Island. Orazio was twelve years Maria's senior, not so unusual in those days. At only fifteen she had left her entire family behind in Sicily and was embarking on an arduous adventure to a new country with a new husband. She was frightened, but Orazio was an honest, gentle, and caring husband who did not impose himself on her until she was prepared to be a "wife." Orphaned at twelve, Orazio's wife and children would become the center of his universe.

After a long day at the store, Connie began walking home through the narrow alleys that connected large apartment buildings to the main street. The streets were little more than alleys, floored unevenly with cobble and absent of any florescence. Brick and concrete fortified the neighborhoods. From an occasional crack in the concrete, a tree would try to sprout, but they were even bereft of foliage. As she began to climb the steps to her apartment, her brother Sam hollered from the window.

"Hey, Connie. There's a phone call for ya."

Hmm, she thought. She wasn't expecting a call and had told her girlfriends that she had planned on staying home for the evening. She was still unsteady from the night before. The spinning of her feet on the dance floor and the spinning thoughts inside her head had left her exhausted, but her anticipation heightened as she reached for the receiver.

"Hello," she said.

"Hi, it's Frank. I just wanted to see what you were doing tonight."

"Tonight?" she asked.

"Yeah, why not?"

"Well, it's already dark, and it's awfully cold. I heard they're expecting more snow."

"C'mon," he said. "We'll go to the movies. It'll be warm and dry in there."

Connie looked in the mirror. Excitement and uncertainty flashed back. She looked weary from work and would need some time to prepare. She was silent for a moment. "Fine," she finally said. "Six thirty. No later. I'm at 77 Wall Street."

"I know where you are. See you then." The receiver went dead.

Connie hoped to be gone by the time her parents arrived home from the store. She didn't want to explain who she was with or where she had gone, but she would leave them a vague note. She had never lied to her parents, but these were foreign feelings for her.

Frank arrived right on time—a good sign, Connie thought. Her hands were shaking as she put on her gloves.

"Are you cold already? We haven't even gone outside yet."

"Oh no. I'm fine." *Damn*, she said to herself. *What am I doing?* With one more glance in the mirror and a smoothing of her hair, she shut the door behind them and followed Frank as he helped her down the stairs. *A gentlemen too*, she thought. *This may work out after all.*

They went to see that new movie starring Humphrey Bogart and Ingrid Bergman, the one all the papers were talking about. Connie sat stiffly, hands folded tidily in her lap, eyes dashing forward. Occasionally she would glance sideways toward Frank. His was a sly, almost sinister grin that could melt the heart of any reluctant woman, and the deep ebony depths of his flashing eyes were maelstroms into which a woman could fall hard, not knowing where she was falling. He had gentle hands anchored to strong arms. His black hair glistened.

It had begun to snow harder as Frank escorted Connie through the streets toward the train station. Her shoulders brushed his as they splashed across the street in the sheeting snow. The eleven o'clock train was running late, which meant they would be standing at the station for another hour, each wondering what they would talk about. As Connie was getting wet on the street, makeup running, she realized she would miss her curfew. Finally, at midnight, the train arrived. They entered the train and sat toward the back for privacy. Connie moved a wisp of hair that hung damply on her forehead.

"I must look awful," she said.

"No, you look beautiful, even wet," Frank replied.

Connie felt her face warm.

"Did you like the movie?" Frank asked.

"Yes, very much."

She waited for him to add something more. When he didn't, he glimpsed a spark of disappointment in her eyes.

With resounding silence, they arrived at their destination and disembarked. Connie's pace quickened as she glanced at her watch.

"I'm thirty minutes late, and I never told my parents I was going out with you."

"Are you glad you did? They were in the hallway of the building now. When she didn't respond, he took her face in his hands and set his mouth on hers. There was nothing gentle or undemanding about his kiss. She fought against it, trying to pull back, but eventually succumbed. With that kiss, he just walked away. Connie stood for a moment trying to collect herself, wondering what her parents would think of her behavior. It was so out of character. Then she opened the door.

The slap was hard and unexpected. She had never even been spanked by her father. He never hollered at her. Orazio's large body loomed in the entryway. He didn't speak, just turned sharply on his heels and lumbered through the tiny hallway to his bedroom. Connie stood frozen in the kitchen, her cheek singed. Just then, Maria opened the door of the bedroom and came into the kitchen. She was pointing a finger.

"You had your father crazy. He was so scared. His face was red like the sun. He's in the room now with tears. He feels so bad for hitting you, but you were late, and he didn't know where you were, or with who."

"Mama," Connie said. "I didn't know the train would be late because it wasn't snowing much when we went into the theatre."

"Yeah, whose we"?

"Me and Frank.

"Frank Tullio?" Maria asked.

"Yes."

Maria gave Connie a stern look. "But he's poor."

That following Monday, Frank Tullio received his draft notice in the mail. It was November 15, 1942.

Chapter 5

Frank was dispatched for four years. The first two years he was in the States, and the last two he was stationed in Belgium, Holland, England, and France. He rose quickly in rank to sergeant.

When he was drafted, Frank and Connie were not formally considered a "couple." They had been out on a few very memorable dates. They began writing to each other, and on occasion Frank would call. The longer he was away from Connie, the more he was enticed by the thought of her. He never really cared much about any of his former girlfriends; that just wasn't his style, and in fact he had decided years before not to pursue a serious relationship. He watched as his friends were getting married at twenty-one or two, and he thought they were crazy. He still wanted to play the field, yet he frequently found himself thinking of Connie when he least expected it. More than once, his mind had drifted, and he would imagine her standing by his bunk smiling at him while he slept. These images bewildered him, but they wouldn't stop.

One night after mess hall, Frank was lying in his bunk reading about Willie and Joe in "The Stars and Stripes" comic strip. He yearned for some humor tonight, but he could not shake the empty feeling he had. Below was his buddy from home, Joe Saracena. Frank had only been reading for a few minutes, but couldn't remember what he had read. He paused, put down the newspaper, and pulled his wallet from his knapsack. Taking a photo from his wallet, he looked at it briefly and handed it down to Joe.

"So, what'ya think?" Frank asked.

"Wow, she's a looker. I'll marry her! Where did ya find her?"

"I met her at a dance hall. She's actually a friend of my little sister, Mary. I can't seem to get her out of my mind."

Frank lowered his eyes to the photo and managed a slight smile.

The following day was Saturday, and the guys had the day off. They were stationed at Ft. Monmouth in New Jersey. They had decided to drive into the city for the evening. While in Times Square, they would hit a few bars and wear off some pent-up energy. Frank was with his buddies, Joe Saracena, Mike Hardy, and Al DiMattio. They drove slowly through the square, canvassing every bar and restaurant, then pulled up in front of an exclusive looking establishment with a black and gold awning and two elaborate gold gilded lions flanking the door.

"Hey, let's try this place. It looks nice," Mike said.

"Okay," they replied in unison.

The club was cheerfully noisy, thick with shouted conversation. They strutted into the bar like peacocks, removed their hats, and searched for a table from which they could see the stage easily. Joe, Al, and Frank began drinking beers. Mike was already shooting down whiskey shots. On the stage there was an upright piano and nothing else. The crowd was mixed in age and gender. They were all dressed in fine clothes or, if in the service, a neatly-pressed uniform. The behavior of the crowd fit their attire.

Shortly after nine o'clock, a stocky gentleman took to the stage, followed by a lovely young woman. The gentleman took the microphone and introduced himself and his partner. Her name was Sally.

"She's really cute, huh," said Mike.

"Yeah, kind of a girl next door, wholesome, all apple pie and ice cream cute," Joe added.

Sally was petite, with auburn hair, green eyes, and freckles. She was dressed in a red peplum waist jacket with a matching skirt that fell just below the knee and a string of pearls that choked at the neckline of her jacket. She stood next to the piano touching it with her legs, put the microphone to her lips, and began to sing.

The guys all stood at immediate attention, their mouths gaping and eyes bulging. This girl had the voice of a vixen, slow and sultry, her body moving in harmony. The howling began, and the hats were waving above their heads. They couldn't take their eyes off Sally. Mike was still shooting down the whiskey, his eyes glued to her, when all of a sudden he leaped from his chair, crashing onto the stage. Sally staggered back to avoid being hit by Mike's massive body. He grabbed at her ankle, as Al, Frank, and Joe watched in horror. What on earth was he doing? Was he crazy or just intoxicated? They knew the answer. He was wildly intoxicated and mildly crazy. In what seemed like seconds, the racket brought about half dozen men pouring onto the stage, where they wrestled Mike out of the door and onto the sidewalk. The guys followed behind shaking their heads in embarrassment.

"You stupid ass," Frank yelled. "Now you got us kicked out because you're a drunk. You Irish, you all drink too damn much!" He glared at Mike. "Yeah, you jerk," Joe added.

"We can go someplace else," Mike slurred.

"Are you crazy? You stupid bastard, you can't even stand up," Al hollered.

"Let's just go back to the barracks. I'll drive," said Frank, but Mike wouldn't hand over the keys.

"I can drive. I drive like this all the time. I'm not drunk. You guys are just too sober," he said laughing.

Reluctantly, they all got in the car.

Heading south toward Trenton, the roads were dark and winding. They had a midnight curfew, and at 10:30, they would be cutting it close. It was a midsummer's evening, and the air was still warm and moist from the heat of the day. Before long, Joe and Al were asleep in the back seat, induced into a deep slumber from the thickness of the air and the beer. Frank kept close watch up front. Thirty minutes or so into the trip, Frank noticed Mike's eyes beginning to flutter. He started to weave and drifted toward the rail.

"Hey, Mike. You need to pull over now and let me drive."

Mikes head tossed and straightened. "I'm okay," he slurred. "Take a nap with the guys and I'll have us back before you can say 'Sally.'"

"No," Frank ordered, his heart pounding. "Pull over now!"

"You're not sergeant yet, Frankie, so just relax."

Frank watched as the road took another turn and the right side of the truck tilted slightly off the asphalt. Up ahead, the guardrail was sturdy enough, but beneath it the cliff looked unforgiving. Frank knew that fatigue and alcohol caused accidents. If he didn't react at the right moment, see what was about to happen, and lunge to push Mike out of the way, they would go over the edge.

Frank grabbed the wheel, gripping it hard. "What the hell are you doing?" Mike screamed. Joe and Al woke to the commotion and saw Frank clamoring for control. Finally, Frank succeeded, swerving violently to the left. The front right tire hit the rail, and the car came to an abrupt stop.

"Didn't you see that guardrail?" Frank shot back.

The following morning, Frank went outside to use the privy. It was still dark. He stripped off the clothing he had slept in and turned on the shower. With his hands grasping the sides of the wall, he let the water course over his head. He thought about what had happened to him just hours before, and he thought about her. He stood for some time, then turned off the shower and dressed. Now fully clothed and bathed, he knocked on the door of the sergeant's quarters. He stood at attention as the door opened. The sergeant stood aside so Frank could enter. It was a small room with one paneled window. A table with one chair and a single lamp held a pitcher of what appeared to be water and a newspaper. There was a low bookcase, empty, along one wall adjacent to a small desk. Underfoot the floor was bare, except for some torn linoleum.

"All right, Frank, why don't you tell me why you're here?" sergeant asked.

"Would you oblige me by giving me a weekend pass for next weekend?" He took out the photo of Connie and handed it to the sergeant. "I have some personal business to attend to at home."

The sergeant smiled affably. "Sure."

Connie heard the bell of the train approaching the station and went to the platform. The station master came out as the doors were clattering open. She looked down the platform, where people were collecting and greeting those waiting. Then she saw Frank, and he saw her. Making his way through the crowd, he finally reached her, gripped her tightly, and said, "Will you marry me?"

Frank was dispatched to Europe during the last two years of his duty. During this time, Connie spent much of it planning her wedding. It all seemed surreal, as she wondered if she even knew the man she had agreed to marry. She was certain of one thing. There was an attraction between them that could not be denied.

Connie had envisioned this day as a little girl, and she wanted the finest dress money could buy. Only in New York would this be possible. The train ride to New York City was uneventful. She had never ridden the train such a distance alone, and Orazio was apprehensive about letting her go, but she assured him she would be fine. She read women's magazines, raising her eyes on occasion to observe the crowd. Most of the trip, she kept her eyes low, and at times wanted to disappear as a large group of servicemen pierced right through her with their stares. She could feel their eyes, hot on her skin. She glanced up, then away again. She shifted her body and held the magazine closer to her face.

When after several hours the train came to a full stop, Connie disembarked and looked down the platform in both directions. She had not seen her cousins since she was a small child, but they had a current photo of her. Almost immediately, a younger woman about her age and an older woman approached. The older woman said, "Connie?"

"Jenny?" Connie asked.

The older woman extended her arms. "Yes, honey. Give me a hug. This is your cousin Arlene. I know you don't remember her."

Arlene didn't look like her cousin. She was dark haired and skinned. Her features were more pronounced. The two young women embraced.

"Cmon, Uncle Johnny is in the car waiting for us," Jenny said.

They shuffled off into the crowds with Connie's over-sized luggage swinging by her side.

Uncle Johnny really wasn't her uncle. Jenny was a cousin, and Uncle Johnny was related by marriage. Like Orazio, he was big and boisterous, happy go lucky, and full of charm.

"Hey, little Connie, not so little anymore," Uncle Johnny laughed. "Here, honey, let me take your bags. You sit back there with the girls. I'm the chauffeur today."

Into the heavy traffic Uncle Johnny drove until they arrived in Queens. As Connie opened the door and looked up and down the street, she took a long breath and thought, *This is where I would like to live.* The houses were not connected. Each one had its own private yard and single driveway. They looked the same but were different in color. Some had a stone or brick front, while others were wood. They all had an A-frame gable with a portico. She knew Uncle Johnny did not make more money than her father, and she couldn't understand why she still lived in an apartment. *When I am married, I will live in a house like this,* she thought. *Frank will agree.*

Connie and Frank's families lived in a neighborhood called the West End. It was a primarily Italian enclave where there were no owners, only occupiers. A person's house was not the same status symbol for the West Enders that it was for most middle-class people. Making a good impression was important, but people were more interested in an individual's moral qualities and friendliness than the house he or she lived in.

The following afternoon, Connie, Jenny, and Arlene rode into Brooklyn with Uncle Johnny driving. Jenny didn't drive, and Connie wondered if Uncle Johnny had a job. They stopped in front of Kleinfields, a premier bridal shop.

"The rich and famous shop here," Jenny said.

"Well, I'm not rich or famous, but I am buying my gown here."

After trying on only one gown, Connie fell in love with a gorgeous ivory slip of satin floor-length gown. The dress was beautiful, and the ivory satin fit her torso perfectly. It had a high neck and was sheer from the upper bodice to the neckline. There was a delicate ruffle at the top of the bodice, and the waist was fitted. The remainder of the gown was a very simple satin with a stiff underlay and a very long train. The veil she chose was also simple and sheer, with a small cap of lily of the valley.

"This is it, Jenny."

"It is stunning, Connie, but have you looked at the price tag?"

"Yes, it's fine. Papa said whatever I want, he will pay for."

"Oh, I hope that new husband of yours proves to be as extravagant as your father," Jenny said, laughing. "I heard from your mother that your wedding will be the talk of the town, no expense spared. Boy, that father of yours."

Connie just nodded her head in affirmation.

Chapter 6

Connie knew that there are some things that one hesitates to bring down into words, but the words were knocking at her lips.

"Frank, I need to talk to you about something important."

They had just returned home from their honeymoon in the Poconos days before, and she was feeling invigorated.

"Sure, blue eyes," Frank replied.

Connie laughed. Her eyes were not blue, but green.

"Is everything okay?"

"Yes." She adjusted her posture, folded her hands, and set her eyes squarely on his. "Frank, you know how smart your teachers always said you were, especially in math."

"Yeah."

"You have a brilliant mind and a sharp tongue. You're one of the few boys I know who graduated from high school. You don't speak or look like an average Italian. You never use slang. You need to go to college, and the GI Bill will help get you through. I will work to support us while you're getting the education that should be yours. You deserve it. We both do."

Frank straightened his shoulders and bore his eyes into Connie.

Have my wife support me? What will people think? Frank Tullio isn't good enough for Connie Savaca. That's what everyone thinks anyway, isn't it?"

The question was preemptory, requiring an answer. When Connie didn't respond right away, Frank flashed a look of annoyance. This was their first confrontation, and she wasn't as prepared as she had thought. "I don't mind," she said, lowering her voice. "I'm a very good seamstress, and I can make good money. My parents will help us. It won't be for that long, Frank."

"No," he said emphatically. "I will get a better job, and there will be no need for you to work. I won't have my wife working." Off to bed he stormed.

Connie slumped in her chair and wrung her hands. She had grown up getting almost everything she asked for. This would not be the case with her new husband. So much for the honeymoon, she thought.

Before the war, Frank had worked in the press room of a local printing company. When he returned home from the war, they agreed to take him back. The money was not very good, and the chemicals they used hung heavily like a poisonous cloud, but it was a job. Many evenings Frank came home coughing and wheezing. This wasn't a job he planned on keeping, he thought to himself almost daily.

Connie and Frank rented a quaint apartment in a small wood-shingled duplex in the outskirts of the city. The front yard was small but manicured, with hedges of evergreen and wisps of rose crawling the white fence like a conquering snake. This home resembled Jenny's in New York. Connie thought the rent was too high for their budget, but Frank said that if she wanted it badly enough, he would find a way to pay for it. Connie was comforted by this home, and she particularly liked the front farmer's porch and rocker. It was July, and the sidewalks were blazing, the heat puffing white billows in indistinguishable shapes. Connie was sitting rocking in the chair when Frank arrived home from work. He walked slowly up onto the porch and gave her a gentle kiss on her cheek. Rocking methodically in the chair, she seemed deep in thought. So was he. He spoke first.

"I got laid off today."

She didn't flinch or even look up. "I'm pregnant."

Connie's pregnancy was not unusual. She had the expected morning sickness during the first trimester and the usual swelling and discomfort toward the end. She had worked as a seamstress for the entire term, but working full time at a factory in a stationary position all day was unforgiving on her body. When she returned home in the evening, she was usually irritable and uncomfortable. All she wanted to do was get into a nice warm bed and not move, but being a good wife, she would cook a full dinner and clean the dishes while Frank sat and read the newspaper.

All the troops were home now, and there were a glut of workers competing for the same jobs. Frank was looking, but perhaps not hard enough, Connie thought. He didn't posses any one specific skill and wasn't trained in a required discipline. However, he was as sharp as a tack and meticulous about detail. He would be a good point man at any company, but the companies did not come calling, and with the delivery approaching, the tension between the two escalated. On Saturdays, Connie would go to her parents' store, where they would stock her up on enough groceries for the week. Orazio had added fruits and vegetables to his fish market in recent years. Although Frank was very appreciative and thought the world of his in laws, he undoubtedly felt worthless and guilty. His own parents made no attempt to help their son and his pregnant wife, and he knew better than to ever expect it. He wondered about the old country, where a man's son followed into his father's profession. Was this a matter of convenience, or were some people predisposed to certain kinds of work? Were some people actually born to be laborers and others doctors? Were we born with a finite aptitude; was the opportunity to achieve predetermined as well? He hoped not.

Connie went into labor on March 14, 1947. Her delivery would be especially difficult. Her doctor was not a specialist but rather an incompetent general practitioner. She should have had a cesarean section. Instead, she clenched her teeth, screaming out occasionally for thirty-eight hours. It was a much longer ordeal than anticipated, and the process left both Connie and the child with visible damage. As a result of the doctor's forceps, the baby, a six-and-a-half-pound boy, emerged with his left eye crushed closed and the same side of his head dented.

The baby came out crying. It was no wonder he wasn't screaming after the task of trying to exit the narrow birth canal. Philip Frank Tullio had struggled coming into this world, and Connie was torn badly as well. She was hemorrhaging and beginning to lose consciousness on the delivery table. It took a full hour for the doctor to contain the bleeding and begin stitching the deep, jagged tears inside her. Finally she was transferred to the recovery room, where mother and son were reunited. The swaddled baby was handed to Connie, and she tried to soothe him, ignoring the pain in the entire lower half of her body. She kissed his little face.

"Look at you. You're beautiful," she cried, holding little Philip tightly against her chest. His heart seemed to beat in rhythm with hers. He was the image of his mother, with fair skin, wisps of golden hair, and lightly colored eyes. Finally Frank was allowed to enter the room. He stood in the distance for a moment and stared.

"Come closer, Frank."

Frank watched Philip burrow himself into the front of Connie's hospital gown, making small, voracious noises.

"Are you hungry?" Connie asked the baby. "Is that why you're whimpering?"

Just then a stocky nurse entered the room. Her stoic response came quickly.

"Let him cry. A baby shouldn't be fed every time it cries. They get spoiled if they're not kept on a schedule."

"Then he'll be spoiled," Connie coldly replied.

As though the baby knew what his mother was thinking, the whimpering became a shriek, punctuated by gasping gulps of air. Finally Frank wakened out of his trance and walked closer to Connie and the baby. He looked scornfully at the nurse.

"Get my wife a bottle. She would like to feed my son. Now!"

The nurse acquiesced. Philip's small mouth clamped down firmly on the bottle, sucking with mindless appetite. Frank said nothing further. When the nurse closed the door behind her, he sat down in the chair next to the bed and quietly watched Philip feed. Eventually, he came even closer, still with that edgy look on his face. When Philip had stopped feeding and was falling off to sleep, Connie handed him to Frank and said, "Here's your son." With his face still blank, he looked down at his son and kissed him tenderly. Within a few minutes, this child was his.

It would be a week before mother and son were released. Connie was discharged to bed rest.

"What mother rests with a newborn?" she asked her doctor as he was signing her discharge papers.

"Well, try to get as much rest as possible. You've been through quite an ordeal."

"Yes, and why was that, I wonder," Frank said, inching closer to the shrinking doctor. With that, the doctor walked toward the door and closed it firmly behind him.

"Hmm," said Frank. "A bum, a real bum. I should sue him."

"Calm down, Frank. Philip's eye will be better in a few weeks, and I am already feeling better."

"What a bum," he said again.

Money was tight, but Connie knew how to stretch it. She scrubbed her own floors and shopped carefully for whatever food items she couldn't get from her parents' store. She was always looking for bargains, and became a quick study for a young woman who had never had to concern herself with prices before. Connie could not return to work for several months, and Frank still hadn't found a suitable job. Connie had saved a small nest egg to get them by for these first few months after the birth. She tucked it away to be used as she needed. It was hidden well.

Frank thought long and hard about his plan. If it worked, they'd be without financial worries for many months. That would give him enough time to secure employment.

There were few trees in the city, and by late October they were stripped of their leaves. Frank clutched his collar, fastening it tightly under his chin. It was unusually cold for October, and without money for a car, he was forced to walk almost everywhere. He reached Buddy's house at 10:00. Connie and the baby were sound asleep when he crept silently out of the house. She would never know he was gone. Thrusting his hand into his right pocket, he gripped the money. Frank had been nicknamed "Lucky Frankie" while in the army. He needed all that luck now.

"Hey, Frankie. Have a seat," Buddy said. "This seat's the lucky one. We've been keeping it warm for you."

"Thanks. Right now I need all the luck I can get. I got a wife, a new baby, and I can't find work. I've been everywhere."

"Maybe you should try looking outside the city limits, in the suburbs. I hear there's more work out there," said Joe.

"Yeah, I've heard that too. The suburbs sound good."

"Yeah, get us all out of this hellhole," said Buddy. "Hey, Gina, bring us some beers, would'ya honey?"

"Sure, Buddy," Gina answered.

Gina and Buddy had been married for two years. She had finally accepted the fact that her house was "the gambling house." They had no children, but when they did, things would have to change. All she asked was that the guys told their wives where they were.

"Frankie, does Connie know you're here tonight?" Gina asked.

"Sure, Gina."

Joe dealt the cards, and they all looked at their hands. One by one they folded. No one even raised. Frank won the first hand with two low pairs.

"Well, I'm off to a decent start."

Then his luck turned. The next six hands got much worse. He was raising, and losing. He rubbed the tension at the back of his neck. Hand seven, eight, and nine were no different. Frank had lost more than half the nest egg. A frown puckered his forehead. He exhaled with a long sigh, asked for another beer, and with trembling hands ruffled the hair that fell damply over his forehead. When the clock struck one, Frank stood up, and without saying good-bye, slammed the door behind him. He felt dizzy and disoriented. It was the beer on an empty stomach or the sudden comprehension of his irresponsible deed. At 2 a.m., Connie had woken to Philip's crying just as Frank was slipping through the door. She heard the footsteps creeping down the hall.

"Where have you been?" she asked, standing in the hallway with the baby in her arms.

With his back arched and his head cocked, he replied, "Feed the baby and go to bed. We'll talk in the morning. It's been a long night."

"Talk to me now," she demanded.

"Fine, you want it now, I'll give it to you now. It's gone, all of it. Every penny."

He slammed the bedroom door. She followed him with Philip still in her arms. There was no looking back, she thought. She had to look forward. Whatever had happened between her and Frank had to be let go. They had created a life.

"What are you thinking?" he asked, looking up at her from the bed.

"I'm thinking what a goddamn fool you are."

Connie slammed the door behind her, got a pillow and blanket from the closet, and slept on the floor next to Philip's crib.

Connie never confided much in Maria. She was an immigrant with old fashion ideas and values, and she would never understand Connie's feelings. Fortunately, she had a godmother who was closer in age and born in America.

Anna was a secretary, which impressed Connie. She was fashionable and even discussed going to college. Connie didn't know any girls that went to college, or even aspired to. In fact, only fifteen percent of the girls in the West End graduated from high school. Connie was not one of them.

A few days after the gambling incident, Connie was surprised by an unexpected visit from Anna. The doorbell rang, and Connie shuffled to the door dressed in a housecoat, with a bottle in hand, no makeup, and her hair tousled.

"You look awful," her godmother remarked as she handed Connie a beautifully wrapped package.

"Come in, Anna. Why didn't you call?"

"I wanted to surprise you!"

"Well, you certainly surprised me." Connie gestured Anna toward the kitchen.

"No, no, I want to see that beautiful son of yours. Do you think I came to see you?" Anna was always humorous, and Connie could have used some humor right about now.

"I'm sorry I didn't call you sooner to come and see the baby, but it has been so hectic around here."

"Not to worry," Anna said. "I'm not offended, and you know I am very good at inviting myself." Connie laughed, but not heartily. Anna's eyebrows raised.

"Let's go into the kitchen. You can hold Philip while I open this lovely looking package."

"Okay, darling," Anna said.

Connie eyed the box wrapped in blue and white polka dots. "Now what could this be?" she asked, her voice a bit more lighthearted.

She unwrapped the box and found an adorable blue pram with a hood. "Oh, it's so cute Anna. Thank you."

"There's another smaller box tucked inside, Connie."

"Oh, this smaller one was hiding."

She opened the box. Inside was a book titled *My Life*. Connie flipped slowly through the pages. There were pages for photos, pockets for souvenirs, and journal pages in a scrapbook form. The book began in infancy and extended into adulthood. The last section was called "Entering Adulthood."

"Oh my," Connie said. I'm sure we will have plenty to add to these pages. I love it. Thank you, Anna."

"Anytime. I thought little Philip would want to add to this book someday. I'm sure he will a very blessed child. After all, he has you for a mother. He couldn't be luckier."

"Thank you, Anna. That's sweet of you," Connie said as her bottom lip began to quiver. Anna came closer.

"What's wrong, honey? You know you can tell me anything."

Connie wiped her nose which had began to run. "It's Frank. He's a good father, he really is. He loves Philip. I'm just not sure he's a wonderful husband," she said softly.

"He's not mean to you, is he?"

"Oh God, no. He's just so damn frustrated. He doesn't seem to understand sensitivity. He's passionate, and I think he loves me—the letters he wrote to me when he was at war were so endearing—but now he seems different, more removed," she said with sadness in her eyes.

"I try so hard to please him. I clean, cook, take care of the baby, and never burden him with anything."

"Look, you both have been struggling with money problems. I'm sure that has caused him to be cynical. He'll come around honey, just give him some time," Anna said, smiling wide.

"We had a big fight the other evening. I don't ever remember my parents arguing."

"Connie, your parents are unique. Most couples argue now and then."

"You know, now that I think of it, when he courted me he always said, 'I love you,' but even then it was written, never spoken."

"Some men just aren't good at telling you how they feel. It's an emotional thing. Some men think it makes them less 'manly' if they're too sentimental. They want to be in control."

"How do you know so much about men?" Connie asked.

"I've known a few," she said with a wink.

"Funny how sentimental he once was," Connie said in a whisper, lowering her head.

"Well, let's think about this for a moment. If you were thousands of miles away from your fiancée, and didn't want her to stray, wouldn't you make your intentions crystal clear? He doesn't have to try as hard now. Don't you let him get away with it," Anna said, pointing a finger at Connie.

Just then the doorbell rang. It was Maria with a cooked meal in hand. "I have food for you," she said, entering the house.

"Come in, Mama." Everyone kissed.

"How are you Maria?" Anna asked.

"Good. I come to bring food and to pray."

"Pray, for what, Mama?"

"I light candle and pray for Frank to find a job."

"Oh." Connie glanced over at Maria with a grin. "Mama, you don't need to do that."

"I bless the house, throw out the *malocchio*, and pray some more," she said in a determined don't-argue-with-me tone.

"Fine, if you must."

Anna had a smirk on her face. Maria went into the kitchen and retrieved a small bowl from the cupboard. She set the bowl on the table and pulled up a chair. Then she added three drops of olive oil and one drop of water. When the oil and water began to conjoin, she started praying in Italian. Connie and Anna stood still, shooting furtive glances at each other.

When Maria was done, she proceeded to Philip's room, bent over the crib, gave him a big kiss, and walked toward the door. "Okay, I'm done. God bless." And off she went as quickly as she blew in.

Anna broke into uproarious laughter when the door closed. Connie looked seriously at Anna and said, "She really believes in that stuff."

"You're kidding."

Frank came home later that day. The house was quiet. He had borrowed a friend's car and driven south to the suburbs for an interview at a printing company that had connections to his old company. Connie heard him approach. His footsteps were quick and light. As he opened the door, he popped his face in. A grin spanned its diameter. "I did it," he said. "I got a job, a pretty good one."

Speechless, Connie dropped the casserole.

Chapter 7

Frank began work as a production planner in a well respected printing company in Hanover. He was comfortable with the amount of responsibility his position required. He managed what he needed to during the day, but when he returned home at night, the job didn't come through the door with him. That suited him perfectly.

As the production planner, Frank had the opportunity to preview new books before production. If he found a book he liked, he would take home the sample and return it at a later date. He preferred books about history, government, or science. Frank believed fiction was irrelevant. He read voraciously, absorbing all the knowledge he could, and transformed himself into an intellectual, cultured man.

Frank had barely walked in from work this evening when Philip came running." Up, Daddy, up," he squealed.

"Okay, up," Frank said as he lifted his son into his arms. He smelled the aroma of chicken cacciatore streaming through the house. Connie was a fabulous cook. Orazio had taught her well. Frank savored the good food and appreciated every morsel. When the family sat down for dinner, they ate. There was no room for conversation at the table, and Frank wasn't one to make small talk. Unless something important had happened, he spoke only when necessary. The house was quiet, except when Frank was at work, when Connie would turn up the radio and dance with little Philip in her arms.

Today Connie had planned a short vacation on Cape Cod for the three of them to celebrate Frank's new job. She began to fill Frank in on the details of the trip when the telephone rang. She got up and answered it. "Hello," Frank heard her say. "Sure, he's right here." Connie extended her hand for Frank to grab the telephone.

"Who is it?" he whispered.

"I don't know, but the voice sounds wretched." Frank grabbed the receiver.

"Hello," he said. "Oh my God. I'm so sorry."

Connie heard the click of the receiver on the other end before Frank had hung up. He held the receiver in mid air, then very slowly returned it to the cradle.

"What is it?" she asked.

"That was Mike Hardy, you remember Mike from my unit. The Times Square Story."

"Oh yes," Connie said.

"I was supposed to be in his wedding in September."

"Yes, I remember."

Frank looked at Connie, mouth open, his expression bordering on disbelief. "He drove his car into a tree last week and killed his fiancée." Frank picked up the newspaper, walked into the living room, and left his food behind.

***

It came out of nowhere. Frank saw the sky turning black. Just a few minutes before, it was bright and clear with the sun beating down. With his heartbeat accelerating, he gathered the clam bucket and rake and tossed them hastily into the boat. *Damn*, he said to himself, the catch had been good. He wanted one more bucket, but he knew it would take him at least fifteen minutes to row back to the other side of the spit, toward the bay, and away from the open sea. He looked out and felt a sense of dread. He didn't like the feeling and tried to shirk it off. His legs became rubbery as he sat in the center seat and rapidly began to row. The fog was thickening and draining the world of color. The sky exploded, and suddenly rain the size of golf balls began pelting down on his bare back. The ocean was a big place, and in it Frank felt like a tiny spot.

The boat was small. He should have rented a vessel fitted with a small engine rather than a rowboat that would not be stable or reliable in a storm. But who would have anticipated the drastic change in the weather pattern? Frank was not a seafaring man, and he was certainly no match for a mountain of water driven by an angry wind. The boat began rocking forward and back. *Just get me back*, he thought, willing his arms to move faster. He rowed feverishly until the sweat was pouring down his face along with the rain. He sensed he was losing his grip both physically and emotionally. Desperate to remain steady, he placed his feet into position for greater leverage and rotated the oars again. Lighting. Thunder. He rowed faster, the effort exhausting. Then it happened. He lost his breath for a brief moment, and that lapse caused him to lose an oar into the cantankerous sea. The sea had a mind of its own, and it had a vengeance for Frank.

Frank could not swim. Connie had tried to teach him numerous times, but he was stubborn.

"I'm not gonna have my wife teach me how to swim. I'm a grown man, for Christ's sake," he would say.

He thought about screaming for help, but he was too far out for anyone to hear him. So, he just sat and thought about his actions, his wife, his son, and his carelessness.

Back on shore, Connie used her forearm to wipe the perspiration from her face. She took a deep breath, held it for a moment, and exhaled as she stared out at the water. When they had arrived, there were throngs of people scattered in clusters on the shore, but they'd taken note of the clouds and were now gone. The descending clouds were invading, and the fog was becoming dense. Connie sighed and checked her watch. It was almost five o'clock. She threw on a sweater, and placed a blanket over little Philip, who was asleep on the sand beside her. It had been a long day at the beach. The cooler had been depleted of food long ago, and Frank had decided to dig for a few dozen quahogs to bring back to the cottage. Connie sat rigid in her chair, gazing toward the horizon. The clouds looked ominous. Frank should have been back by now.

The last of the lifeguards were just packing up. She watched as the waves picked up. Painted buoys were bobbing, and moored boats were rocking harshly. She could wait no longer. She jumped up and ran toward the guard station.

"Excuse me," she said breathlessly. "I have a problem. I'm very worried, because my husband set off at about two o'clock in a rowboat. He said he planned on rowing to the other side of the narrow spit. He should be back by now."

The young, burnished lifeguard appeared slightly anxious. "I'm sure he's fine, ma'am," he said. "I'll call the harbormaster, and they'll send out a boat to look for him. They'll find him."

Visibly shaken, Connie returned to her chair but could not sit. She gathered Philip up in her arms, trying not to rouse him, and began pacing the beach. She tried to retrace Frank's steps. He had departed from the east end of the beach. She walked toward the bend in the seascape. The water had taken on a gray hue, as the sun no longer shimmered off it. Normally tranquil, the surf seemed to catapult. Philip became restless in Connie's arms. As she was trying to comfort him, she heard someone calling her name. She looked out toward the sea but saw nothing. *Connie, Connie*, she heard. The echo was almost ethereal.

Distraught, not knowing which way to turn next, she ran back to the lifeguard station with Philip now fully awake in her arms.

"Momma, why are we running?" he asked sleepily.

"It's okay, honey. Mommy's just trying to find Daddy. You hush now," she whispered.

At the lifeguard station, the lifeguard was waiting with the harbormaster. They seemed uneasy, which caused her more concern.

"I heard someone calling my name from that direction," she said, pointing east. "It must be Frank," she insisted.

"Ma'am, we are doing everything we can to find him," the harbormaster tried to reassure her. "We have three boats out looking."

She looked at him in disbelief and began to walk the beach again, breaking the sand hard and angry. Then she heard something. It sounded like a motorboat. As it broke the fog, she saw it. It was coming at her fast. She moved to the northern edge of the pier and glanced out across the tide. She squinted and thought she saw three figures on the boat. She prayed that one was Frank. The boat forged ahead quickly. She could see someone who looked like Frank sitting at the back of the boat. Her breathing leveled and her pulse slowed. She ran toward the dock. Trembling from head to toe, Frank was wrapped in a blanket and lifted off the boat into the arms of his wife.

"I heard you calling me," she said, tears rolling down her cheeks. "I heard my name over and over again."

Frank's eyebrows puckered together.

"What are you talking about? I never called your name."

The day Frank bought his first car, a blue 1950 Chevy Bel Air, was also the first day Frank and Connie went looking for a home. It was a mild-April afternoon, the sun splayed from east to west. They had decided on digging their roots into Quincy, a lovely suburb just fifteen minutes south of Boston and twenty minutes north of Hanover, where Frank worked.

As they drove through neighborhoods looking for sale signs on homes, they crested a hill and stumbled upon a brown duplex. It was oddly rectangular and box like, but sited on a lovely street on a well-manicured hill. As they got out of the car together with Philip in tow, Connie noticed a cardinal landing on the tip of a forsythia bush. The bush framed the front side of the driveway. Flapping to stay balanced, the cardinal made a branch sway like a drunken hobo in a boxcar.

"Look at that cardinal, Frank. I love birds. Look at the way it flashes it's wings. They're so carefree. They can just flutter off into the sky whenever they want."

"I've heard that birds on a house are a curse," Frank said.

"Nonsense, and since when do you believe in superstition? Mama's been rubbing off on you, eh?"

"I didn't say I believed in curses," Frank shot back. "I just said that's what I've heard."

"Well, it's ridiculous, and I like the house."

"You do?" Frank asked.

"Yes I do."

"It's not very pretty, and you haven't even been inside."

"Frank, can we knock at the door to see if anyone is home?"

"I guess so," he said, edging near the door. Frank looked the house over, his eyebrows raised at the corners. He approached the front door, knocked, and heard footsteps. An elderly man answered wearing blue jeans and suspenders.

"Yes?" the old man said.

"Good afternoon. I'm Frank Tullio. My wife and I were out driving when we noticed your for sale sign. I know it's presumptuous, but could we come in for a look?"

The old man smiled. "Well, of course you can," he said. "Just hold on a minute while I get my wife. Gertie, there's a nice young couple here that would like to see the house. Are you presentable?"

"Of course I am. Let them in, you old fool."

The old man grinned and rolled his eyes at Frank. "Right this way." He directed Connie and Frank in. "Take a look around," he said with a broad smile.

Just then, the old man's wife walked in. She was plain and slightly heavyset but lovely for an older woman. Her hair was swept up in a simple bun, and she wore no makeup, but it was clear that at one time she was beautiful.

"You folks from around here?" Gertie asked.

"We live in Boston," Connie replied.

"Oh, city folk, eh?"

Connie smiled back. "I suppose."

"Well, this here house sits on farmland that was once owned by the Adams Family, as in President John."

"Oh my. Very historic. Frank loves history."

"Yes. I can name all the presidents in order of service." Frank straightened his head and rolled his shoulders.

Connie noticed the home was unadorned and void of any architectural definition. The rooms were square with old twelve-over-twelves placed in odd locations. There were almost no closets, and Connie realized the reason for this. The house was built in 1920, and at that time, personal belongings were limited to a mere handful of items. One small closet could accommodate an entire family. Frank didn't take notice of the limited closets, as he was too busy inspecting the bathroom. When he returned, he looked at the old man and asked, "How much do you want for it?"

Connie looked at Frank, shocked. This was the first house they had looked at.

"Eleven thousand," replied the old man.

"You've got a deal." Frank extended his hand. Connie looked on speechless. "We'll come back tomorrow with all the necessary papers."

"Right-o," said Mr. Smith, fiddling with his suspenders.

"Our daughter will be happy to have us. Her husband just passed away, and she needs us to help her with the children."

"Oh, I'm sorry," Connie replied.

"Don't be sorry. Everyone dies sometime."

Connie flinched. They walked out slowly, Connie shooting questioning glances toward Frank.

"What was that all about?" she asked.

"What? You said you loved it."

"I said I liked it, but we didn't look at any other homes. I may have loved another house."

"You know I hate to shop," Frank shot back. "And besides, since it's a duplex, your brother Sam can live in the other apartment. He could use some help, and I won't charge him much."

Perhaps he had a point, Connie thought. Sam was newly married and had a mild physical disability.

"Frank, I'm sure my parents will be very grateful." Connie nodded her head and acquiesced, again.

A week after they moved in, they decided to buy Philip a dog. Philip was almost four, and every stray dog in the neighborhood seemed to climb on the toddler's foot, nuzzle its snout into his little calf, and whimper. The touch of Philip's hand would immediately silence the animals. When they entered the pet store, Philip walked straight toward the crate of a black and white border collie.

"Can we take him out, Mommy?"

"Let me ask the nice salesman, honey."

The salesman carefully lifted the twelve-week-old puppy out of his crate and laid him on the floor. The pup could have scampered off, but instead it settled on Philip's foot, his snout nuzzled into Philip's little calf, a whimper emanating from the pup's mouth.

"Oh, Mommy, he's crying. He wants us to take him home with us. We'll call him Tiny."

"That's a perfect name."

CHAPTER 8

Connie was able to quit her job as a seamstress. Philip was in elementary school, and Connie was ready for another child. Frank was perfectly content with having only one child.

"I grew up in a madhouse. Not enough food, too much noise, and not even a small corner to call your own. And forget about love—what was that?" he said.

"I don't want Philip to be alone because you had a miserable childhood. It's not fair to him. And I want another child. Don't you? Maybe a girl, Frank?"

"What's the chance of that happening?" he laughed.

"Well, I'm not sure. Maybe good if we have Mama come over," she said with enticement in her eyes.

"You're kidding," he said.

"It's worked before. We can afford another child, you know we can. Just one more."

"Fine, one more. And if it's not a girl, too bad."

***

You couldn't look at her and not be proud, Dad thought to himself.

"She looks like me," Dad said.

"Hogwash, she looks like me," Mom shot back.

Dad smiled. Actually I was a combination of both my parents, with Mom's green eyes, small nose, and light skin and Dad's full lips and dark hair. They named me Donna, after Donna Reed, Mom's Hollywood icon.

Dad was much more relaxed with his second child. He wouldn't change a diaper, but he would give me a bottle and try valiantly to burp me. Mom would watch Dad as he held me for hours in the comfort of his arms. It warmed her heart and rekindled her love for him. Dad mellowed as he realized that there's no experience quite like having children, and despite the challenges they once faced, he considered himself fortunate because of the family he had helped create.

Money was not as tight as it had been in the past. Dad had proved his value in the workplace and had received many substantial pay raises. Although far from wealthy, we were certainly comfortable. Still, Dad remained cautious with his money, but would give Mom a generous weekly allowance to spend at her discretion. Mom never spent it on herself, but when it came to Philip and me, we always had the finest clothes, the best food, and the newest toys and gadgets. Mom would take us downtown to shop, then out to lunch at Kresges, a department store with a small luncheon counter. It wasn't fancy, but it became our routine, and we felt special. Our friends never went out to lunch with their moms.

When I was five, Mom began inquiring about new homes in the adjacent community, Braintree. For her, the transition to a more upscale town, with better schools, was long overdue.

One evening after dinner before she had washed the dishes, Mom sat down on the sofa next to Dad.

"Yes?" he asked, barely looking up at her from behind his glasses.

"Oh nothing. I thought I would just sit here next to you a moment."

Dad raised his eyebrows but didn't respond.

"What are you reading?" she asked.

"The newspaper."

"Oh, anything good in the classifieds, maybe houses?"

"Houses. Is that what this is all about, houses?"

"Frank, don't you think it's time for us to buy a nice single-family house?"

"What's wrong with this one?"

"I'd like a single family in Braintree. Braintree is a much nicer town than Quincy, and the schools are great. I've never liked this house. It's never felt like home, and it doesn't give me a warm feeling."

"We'll turn on the heat," Dad said sarcastically.

"Frank."

"Connie, what about your brother. He can barely afford the miserly rent we charge him. Where would he go?" Dad asked.

"I can't take care of him my entire life, Frank. I've been his mother since he was a child. I'm not his mother. He has a mother. We can always lend him money as needed. I want a home that is mine, all mine, not to be shared."

Dad continued to read.

"Frank?" Mom asked, her voice rising.

"I'll think about it," he said.

Within a few months, Dad and Mom purchased a summer cottage on Cape Cod. Dad was adamant about retaining the two family home in Quincy, but he thought a compromise would suffice. From that point forward, Mom,

Phil, and I spent every summer vacation at the Cape house. Eventually Mom stopped mentioning the single-family home in Braintree, but she never stopped dreaming about it, and never understood her intense desire to get us all away from the house in Quincy.

***

The snow was falling heavily. The first-floor windows were hidden behind mountains of puffy whiteness, the sun reflecting off the tip of each one.

Philip was outside having a snowball fight with the neighborhood kids. I had just come back from sledding and was hiding in the cabin-sized igloo Philip had created for me in the backyard. He was sixteen, and I was seven. I worshipped him, and he loved me just as much, always making time to entertain or care for me. Mom and Dad were not the outdoorsy types, but occasionally Mom would come outside to take pictures of our escapades in the snow.

At thirty-eight, Mom was still beautiful, her eyes still a vibrant green and her hair a lovely golden chestnut. She was thin, and men still commented about her "great gams." Her skin was flawless. Dad too was aging well. At forty-two, his hair was still black, he had few wrinkles, and he appeared to be in great shape. He was in the golf and bowling leagues at work, but at home he rarely ventured outside except to mow the lawn on occasion.

Mom neither golfed not bowled, but she was a great swimmer. Mom and Dad didn't share many common interests, and many times Dad went his own way with his friends, but at dinnertime and into the evening, he was always at Mom's side. For my mother, these were rich years, years when she felt God's hand laying gently on her.

The front door opened slightly, the snow blocking its passage.

"Philip, there's a phone call for you," Mom shouted.

"I'm coming."

Philip lumbered through the mountain of snow, lifting each leg deliberately. He took his boots off in the porch and went into the kitchen.

"Hello," he said into the receiver.

"Hi, this is Billy. I got a new BB gun today. Do you wanna come over and see it?"

"Let me ask my mom and I'll call you back."

"Okay, I'll be waiting," Billy replied.

Philip walked into the living room and found Mom.

"Mom, that was Billy. He wants to know if I can come over."

"I suppose you can. Just do me a favor first and get your sister into this house."

"Sure, Mom."

Philip put his coat and boots back on and went outside to find me having an imaginary tea party in my igloo.

"C'mon, Mom wants you in the house, and I'm going over to Billy's."

"No you're not," I wailed. "You promised you'd help me build a snowman." Huge tears welled up in my eyes. "You promised. Please," I cried. My nose was running and my lips were quivering.

"Fine." Philip huffed. "I'll call Billy. I guess I can go over tomorrow. I'm sure we won't have any school."

Tomorrow came. The canopy of snow had lifted.

The call came early in the morning, as these calls do. Mom was just finishing some laundry. She caught the phone quickly so we wouldn't wake. It was still quite early, and school had been cancelled.

"Hello," she said.

"Dad walked into the kitchen and found Mom with the telephone still in her hand.

"God, Connie," Dad said. "You look like you've seen a ghost."

Mom was motionless, the receiver clutched to her chest.

"Billy was accidently shot in the face. He's dead."

"Sit down," Dad said. They both sat for a long while, and then heard the shuffling of Philip's feet in the hallway coming toward the kitchen.

"Hi," he said with a deep yawn.

Mom's face was sober and linen white.

"I've just had some bad news."

Philip was horrified, and as word spread throughout the community, everyone was stunned. That day Mom and Dad held us close until the sun was low on the horizon.

At bedtime that evening, I heard Mom and Dad pacing, and Philip tossing around in his bed. He was mumbling. It was another dream that he could not be rid of. Night after night he would wake screaming, wet with sweat, and Mom would rush in to hold him and try to bring comfort. He had had these nightmares for as long as I could remember. This night, the screaming continued.

I was the only one able to sleep, and while I was drifting off, Mom came into my room, bent down and whispered in my ear, "Thank you. You have saved my son," and she gently kissed my cheek. My eyes were closed.

The following day Philip would not come out of his room. Mom had to force him to eat something, and on the day of the funeral, he refused to attend. Mom and Dad extended their sympathies, and Philip's as well. No explanation was needed for his absence.

Several months had passed since Billy's funeral. Philip was lying in bed one evening trying to fall asleep, attempting to eliminate memories of his best friend. As he continued to struggle with sleep, he felt a surge of discomfort. Lying on the edge of his bed, he turned his face toward his mother.

"What's wrong, Philip?"

"Water," he murmured with great difficulty.

"What?" she said. "I can't hear you."

He shrugged, a movement that made him wince. Mom looked him over carefully. She had been up most of the night with him, until a pale sun finally came out. She placed her hand on his forehead.

"No fever," she said.

But a moment later, his eyes began to roll, and his body began to thrash. Sweat was pouring down his cold, clammy face. Mom felt the color drain from her face, and the room seemed to pulsate around her. She ran to the kitchen, reached for the telephone, dropped it, and picked it up again. She searched her mind for Dr. Jacobs's phone number. His nurse answered.

"Hello. Dr. Jacob's office."

"Hello, this is Mrs. Tullio. Something is terribly wrong with my son."

"Hold on, Mrs. Tullio. I'll get the doctor."

Connie held the phone and began to sway. For a moment the world turned black. Then the doctor answered. She came back into focus.

"What's the problem, Mrs. Tullio?"

"My son is thrashing in his bed, and his eyes are rolling. He has not been well most of the evening."

"I'll be there in ten minutes. Keep him from hurting himself." The receiver went dead.

Oh my God, she thought. She ran back to the bedroom.

"Philip … Philip!" There was no response. With his legs and arms splayed over the bed, he appeared to be falling. Just as Mom straightened him, the doorbell rang. She ran to the door.

"Oh, thank God you're here, Dr. Jacobs," she cried.

"Where is he?"

"In here."

He quickly followed in step. Dr. Jacobs placed a hand over Philip's to calm the agitated movement of his fingers. Mom rose and began to pace. Dr. Jacobs was sitting on the edge of the bed, his brows drawn together, as he analyzed the symptoms. He said little but was monitoring Philip's vital signs. When Mom came back into the room, the doctor was giving Philip a shot.

"Insulin," he said. "He's diabetic."

"No he isn't."

"Oh yes he is."

Philip was still thrashing.

The episode began with images flashing in Philip's head—images of Billy lying cold on a basement floor, images of himself in a casket. Like a recurring theme in some demonic symphony, the darkness swept over him. No light, no air.

"Mom, somebody let me out, let me out! Open the lid! I can't breathe," he screamed, but the casket rim was closed tightly. His arms clawed at the rim of the casket, trying to open it. The light dimmed. He reached up again and tried to heave the lid open. It didn't move. Again. He lay panting in the dark. Panic ensued, as the air was thinning.

Then there was an image of his best friend, Tony, wearing a halo and smiling his big, toothy smile. "What are you doing here?" Philip asked Tony. "You shouldn't be here." They all seemed dead, even Tony, who seemed to be soaring somewhere. The assault continued, the images becoming unrecognizable. Finally, the images began to separate, and decrease. He wiggled his fingers, and voluntarily straightened his head. He could feel his body coming back from the abyss. His face, which had been hard and tight, relaxed.

"Philip, honey," he heard. It sounded like Mom.

Too frightened to approach the bedroom, I stood in the doorway and just waved as Philip turned his dampened face toward me. He flashed a weak smile.

"Philip, can you hear me now? I am taking you and your mother to the hospital. Let's get you up," said Dr. Jacobs.

"Philip nodded weakly as they headed toward the door. Balding Dr. Jacobs was looming over him, holding him steady. Oh boy was he scary, Philip thought.

Philip spent the next five days in the hospital. Both Philip and Mom learned how to check his glucose levels, and using an orange they learned how to administer insulin with a syringe. Dad almost fainted the first time he saw Philip give himself an injection, and I turned my head away.

"Frank, I hope we never need you in an emergency," Mom said, grimacing.

"I hope you never need me too."

Tony came to visit Philip in the hospital on the third day. Tony and Philip had been friends since childhood and had become even closer after Billy died. They shared very similar family backgrounds. Both had Italian grandparents on both sides of the family, and both had sisters, but the similarities ended there. Tony's dark eyes, skin, and hair bore a stark contrast to Philip's pale skin, green eyes, and golden chestnut hair. Tony was mischievous and easily communicated with the girls. Philip was quite different. He was well behaved, predictable, and painfully shy around girls. Philip noticed that Tony seemed troubled.

"My number came up," he said. "Just my luck."

"I'm really sorry, Tony."

"Well, you're lucky. They can't send you to Vietnam now," Tony said.

"I guess you could say that. When do you have to report?"

"September thirtieth."

"Wow, only six weeks."

"Yeah, they don't give ya long to prepare," Tony said, almost stumbling into a chair.

"You okay?" Phil asked.

"Yeah, it's kinda weird. I've been really tired lately. Sometimes I feel like I'm gonna black out or something."

"That is weird. I felt just like that before I got sick. Maybe you should go to the doctor. I probably should have told my mother I wasn't feeling well, but I didn't. It was almost too late."

"What do you mean?" Tony asked. "Like you could have died?"

"Yeah, that's what the doctor told us."

"I'll tell my mother when I get home."

They talked awhile longer about Tony's new girlfriend, Ellie, and Philip told Tony about a new girl he had met, Sarah.

***

There was a war that year, as there had been the year before. It was 1968, and the country was in turmoil. U.S. soldiers were dying at an alarming rate. Antiwar protestors had taken to the streets and were visible on most college campuses. Philip attended Wentworth Institute in Boston, where he was studying to be an engineer. Like Dad, he had an amazing aptitude for math and science.

Philip never had the desire to participate in the antiwar activities, not only because he knew he would not be affected by the conflict but because he was the type of young man who kept his thoughts to himself. This was another trait he inherited from Dad.

On this summery September day, his arrival home had been delayed by the picket line of disgruntled antiwar protesters, and by the time he'd gotten through that, he was already an hour late. As he pulled his new Pontiac GTO into the driveway, Mom was waiting at the door. She had that look on her face again—the look of dread. Philip felt a sinking feeling and a weakening of the knees.

"What's wrong, Mom?" he asked as he slowly walked toward the door. "You've got that look on your face."

"Come in, put your knapsack down on the sofa, and sit down."

"Well?" he asked.

"Philip, Tony's mother has called. He is in the hospital. He is very sick. She didn't get into detail, but she was crying, and Mr. Vacca took the phone when she could no longer speak. It can't be good."

"Maybe he has diabetes." He paused. "Maybe he won't have to leave at the end of the month. That would be good, huh Mom?"

"Maybe," Mom murmured, her eyes piercing the floor.

When Dad arrived home that evening, he suggested that they visit Tony at the hospital. "I don't think he should go alone," Dad said.

"No, you're right," Mom said. "I don't know what to expect after my conversation today. I would feel better if you went with him."

After dinner, they drove the short distance to the community hospital. Neither spoke. When they entered, Dad asked the receptionist where to find Tony's room. Arriving at the door, Philip paused. The familiar smell of ammonia-laden air made him gag.

"Dad, I don't know if I can go in."

"It'll be fine, son. I'm with you. I'm sure it isn't as bad as your mother seems to think it is. You know she overreacts sometimes."

"Yeah, okay, let's go in. I'm fine now."

When Dad opened the door, Tony's family was clustered directly behind it.

"Hello, Philip. Hi Frank," Mr. Vacca called out, standing beside his wife with his arm around her. Dad shook hands with Mr. Vacca and kissed Mrs. Vacca lightly on the cheek. Philip immediately took a seat right next to Tony.

Tony was lying in bed with tubes in his arms. Machines ticked and moaned beside him, but he didn't look sick. He was paler than usual, but he was large and muscular. He was never sick. Philip couldn't remember a day that Tony had missed school, and they had been friends since childhood.

"Hey, how ya doing?" Philip asked.

"I guess okay. I'm just so tired. I can't seem to keep my eyes open, and my neck hurts.

"Maybe you have mono. Too much kissing Ellie," Philip laughed.

Mrs. Vacca forced a smile. For a moment the room was silent. Sometime later, a nurse came in and informed everyone that Tony needed some rest. Dad and Philip said their good-byes.

"I'll be back to see you in a few days, Tony."

"Great, thanks for coming. Thank you too, Mr. Tullio."

Outside the door, Philip took Dad's arm in his. "He's gonna be okay, right Dad"?

"Sure son. He'll be fine."

During the next few days Philip was preoccupied at school and work. When Mom asked him if he planned on going up the hospital to visit Tony, he said," I have so much work. I'll try to get up there soon."

Mom understood by his expression and the tone of his voice that he was scared. At the end of the week, the sound of the telephone startled her as she was sewing a new dress for me. It was Mr. Vacca.

"Connie, it's Tony Vacca."

"Hi, Tony."

"Connie, Tony is asking for Phil. We would like it if he came up to the hospital. Perhaps you should come with him this time."

"Sure," Mom said, squeezing her eyes shut. "I'll bring him up tonight."

"Thanks," Mr. Vacca answered, exhaling into the receiver.

Philip, Dad, and Mom arrived that evening to a much different scene. Philip felt everyone's eyes on him as he approached Tony's bedside.

"Tony wanted to see you before he gets too sleepy," Mr. Vacca said.

Too sleepy? What does that mean? Philip thought. Mrs. Vacca stood and swayed toward the door with her daughters following. Dad spoke quietly with Mr. Vacca.

"Tony, he seems so much worse than when we were here last week," Dad said. "Do they know what is wrong with him?"

"We've known from the beginning, Frank. Tony has leukemia. He's dying."

With that, Mr. Vacca's knees buckled. Dad grabbed him and sat him in a chair in the far corner of the room. Philip spoke with Tony, who acknowledged him by nodding his head. He could no longer speak. Philip made small talk, but his voice was quivering and his hands were knotting on his lap. After a few more minutes, Dad reached for Philip.

"Son, we should go home now. We all need to say goodbye to Tony."

Mom started crying and walked up to Tony's bed. She gave him a tender kiss on the forehead and walked away in tears. Philip wondered what was going on as they walked out the door and into the hall.

On the drive home Philip asked, "Gee, why was everyone crying? Tony's gonna be all right, right Mom?"

Mom and Dad looked at each other in silence. Philip went white.

The following evening, Dad and Philip were at the community hospital playing whist. The hospital sponsored weekly whist games, and the money was donated to the hospital. As they were playing, Philip felt a chill. He could have sworn he heard Tony's voice. It was a fleeting moment, and he questioned it.

They returned home at nine o'clock. Dad settled into his easy chair to read the daily newspaper, while Philip went to his room to study. His homework was almost complete, and Dad was asleep in the chair, when the telephone rang. It was ten o'clock. The sound was jarring. Mom looked over at Dad with a questioning stare and got up to answer it.

"I'm sorry, so sorry," she wailed into the receiver.

Dad stood and walked over to her. He set the receiver back in its cradle.

"Tony's gone," she said. "He died at eight thirty. How do I tell him, Frank? How do I even begin to make sense of it all? First Billy, then the diabetes, now Tony. It's a curse."

"Now stop. There are no curses. Only foolish people believe in that kind of drivel," Dad insisted.

Just then, Philip, dragging his feet and searching Mom's face, came into the room. Mom's bottom lip was quivering, and she shot her eyes to the floor. Dad hunched a shoulder and said, "The war didn't get him. I'm sorry, son."

"It didn't get any of us, Dad," Philip said, choking back tears.

CHAPTER 9

The rest of the year passed quietly enough, but for the usual recurring nightmares, which now included Philip, Tony, Billy, and a small boy who Philip did not recognize. A woman who wasn't clearly visible called out to the boy, who remained in the distance.

"Joey, Joey, where are you," she called over and over again.

It had been ten weeks since Tony died. It was mid-December, and bitterly cold, when a wonderful phenomenon occurred: Philip fell in love.

Philip had never had a serious girlfriend. He was shy around girls in general, but Sarah, animated and lively, brought excitement into his life. Within a year he proposed, and she accepted. Mom and Dad were apprehensive about this decision. At only twenty-one, Philip was far too young to be settling down with anyone, they thought.

"He has no experience with girls," Dad said to Mom.

"You want him to be like you were at that age?" Mom asked with a grin.

"That wouldn't be so bad for him. He needs to sow his oats. He doesn't even know what his oats are yet."

"Rubbish," Mom replied. "You know he's not that kind of boy." Mom twisted the rings on her fingers." I just pray he's made the right choice."

"Yeah, you keep praying," Dad said, rolling his eyes.

Our two families were as different as Sarah and Philip were. Her father was a career military man, a colonel in the army, and he let everyone know it. Boisterous and bold, he liked his scotch, and much to his wife's chagrin, he appreciated a good-looking woman, especially my mother. He commanded a presence in his family, was comfortable in front of crowds, and relished being in the spotlight. His wife was more reserved, seeming to follow in his shadow.

Our family was considerably more low key. Dad was not intimidating and rarely drank. He never looked at other woman. A cultured man, clean cut and gentlemanly, he never spoke a foul word. Dad was loyal to an extreme. The disparity in the family dynamics worried Mom and Dad, but they never mentioned it to Philip. They hoped that the cliché was true: opposites attract.

The year flew by in preparation for the wedding. They were married on a lovely June day in 1969—a full Catholic Mass, followed by a reception at a lakeside country club. The bridal party was large, the bridesmaids wearing peacock blue satin gowns that were quite simple and chic and the groomsmen wearing black tuxedos. Sarah looked lovely, and Philip looked nervous.

After a light buffet luncheon of sandwiches and salads on banquet tables draped with inexpensive white tablecloths, a melancholy settled over me, and I wandered across the grassy knoll to the lake. The sun had finally come out, pale through a light mist, and brought no breeze with it. No ripple broke the water, no sign of a breeze to come. I had just decided to return to the function room, when I heard someone coming up at my back. Philip. Tears welled up in my eyes. I tried to stop the flow.

"Why are you crying?" he asked.

"I'm gonna miss you so much," I stammered,.

"Don't cry," Philip whispered. "It's not like I'm dying or something."

"Oh God. Don't even joke about that," I whimpered. I finally calmed down and tried to convince myself that he would be only thirty minutes away. After they cut the cake and Sarah threw the bouquet, they changed into their travel attire and were gone. Mom and I watched the limousine pull away. When they were barely visible in the distance, Dad finally came out from the building, walking briskly, threading his way purposefully through the crowd.

"Okay, gang. That's that. Shall we go home now and have some real dinner?" Dad bellowed.

I took a breath and looked up at him.

"Sure, Dad," I replied with my bottom lip quivering. I looked over at Mom. With a faraway look in her eyes, she dabbed them gently.

***

After eleven years of marriage, two beautiful sons, a nice home in the suburbs and two good jobs, Philip and Sarah's world began to unravel. It was at this time that their marital problems became evident to our family.

It was just a few weeks before my wedding. The May sky was robin's egg blue, not a cloud in sight, and the air was mild. But I was anxious. I was shopping to pick out a wedding gift for my fiancé, and Philip had come with me to help. I wanted a man's perspective on my choice, and he had impeccable taste in clothes and luxury items. I was driving, and we were sitting in traffic. A semi tractor trailer was directly in front of my car, spewing exhaust. I tried to wedge out into the traffic, but was bottlenecked. I began to gag from the toxic fumes.

"Great, what else can happen today?" I said as I slapped my hand on the steering wheel.

"Calm down," Philip said. "It could be worse. You could be me."

"What on earth does that mean?"

He turned and shrugged his shoulders. His expression was dubious.

"You better make sure you're doing the right thing," he said.

"Why would you say that to me three weeks before my wedding," I replied.

"I just don't want to see you end up like me."

"Like you. What does that mean?"

"Sarah and I haven't been happy for a while." He paused and gazed out the window with a faraway look.

"She acts very cold toward me. I don't think she even really cares."

I turned sharply, my voice blunt. "Look, I am nine years younger than you, and I do know this. You have two beautiful boys. I've heard every marriage has problems at times. Work it out. Mom told me last week that all marriages have their ups and downs. You can't let the down periods consume you. Oh, and by the way, keep it together until after my wedding."

I thought about my last comment and how selfish it was. That would be the first and last time he ever discussed his marital problems with me, but from that point forward, the stress was evident in the way that they looked at each other, and in their words.

By 1984, their world began to come apart. First, their eldest son, Steven, became very ill and was hospitalized for many months with a rare virus called Guillain-Barré. For several weeks, he was in the critical care unit. His recuperation was lengthy. The stress created by this event was overwhelming, and further deteriorated the ill-fated marriage. Soon after their son arrived home to begin the long, arduous rehabilitation process, Philip began having latent complications from his juvenile diabetes.

On a frigid Tuesday morning in February, Sarah, Philip, Dad, and I walked into Dr. Sarif's office with a sense of determination in our souls. Dr. Sarif entered the room in haste, as usual; he was always hurrying to see the next patient. As he sat and reviewed Philip's medical chart, his demeanor instantly transitioned from friendly to stoic and guarded. He began to explain the enormity of the situation.

A feeling of urgency I'd never had before now swept over me. My stomach was knotted, and I seemed to be holding my breath. I looked over at Philip. He looked scared to death and didn't speak, even when the doctor introduced himself to us. Dad was composed, probably in denial, I thought, and I couldn't gauge Sarah's expression at all.

"Do you understand the complexities here?" Dr. Sarif asked us.

I was the only one to respond.

"Yes, I believe so. You are saying that Philip's kidneys are failing, and he has the option of remaining on dialysis indefinitely or having a kidney transplant."

"Well, let me clarify further," he said. "A transplant is by far the most ideal option, preferably from a living, matching donor. The next step is for us to have the potential donors tested to determine whose antigens are most closely matched."

"Does age make a difference?" Dad asked.

"Yes, in some cases. How old are you?"

"I'm sixty-four.

"You are at the far end of the age spectrum; however, if you are a near perfect match, and are in excellent health, you would be a viable donor.

"So, what do we do next?" I asked.

"The next step is for you and your Dad to have your blood drawn. Will Mrs. Tullio be a potential donor as well?"

"No, my wife only has one fully functioning kidney," Dad answered.

"Would you like to know more about the operation itself?" Dr. Sarif asked.

"Not yet," I replied. "What we need to do is see this through one step at a time. We will do whatever it takes.

"Very good," he replied.

Leaving the building in dense silence, Dad and Sarah got into the car first. Philip stopped at the corner and looked at me. His eyes were wet.

"I've always known it would come to this. After Billy and Tony, I knew one day soon, it would get me too."

Three months later, Mom and I sat holding hands and praying that we would have some news soon about Philip and Dad. This was the hardest part—the crushing silence holding us captive in the family waiting area. They were both in surgery simultaneously, Dad's kidney being removed and then quickly inserted into Philip's waiting body.

Dad had been the closest donor match at five antigens versus my three. He never hesitated giving up a kidney for a moment, saying it was a small price to pay in light of what he could lose. Dad was a real hero throughout the long, grueling testing process. A barrage of very invasive and sometimes dangerous tests were conducted on his body for several months to determine his viability. At sixty-four years of age, he would be one of this facility's oldest donors.

I could hear the rumbling in my stomach. Many hours had passed. "Mom, would you like me to go to the cafeteria to get you some food"?

"No, no, I can't eat."

"Mom, you have to eat something."

"No, I don't. But you do. Here, go and get yourself something."

I turned to walk away, and she grabbed at me and stuffed a ten-dollar bill into my pants pocket.

"Okay, Mom. I'll be right back with some food."

Mom bowed her head and sighed.

As we sat into the third hour, a nurse finally approached Mom. She was very cheerful, with a quick step.

"Good news," she said. "Your husband is in recovery, Mrs. Tullio."

"How is he?"

"He did incredibly well. He is quite a character. He had us all laughing."

"Really," I asked a bit surprised. "Dad, a comedian?"

"When he wakes, we will let you see him," she said.

"And my son?" Mom asked.

"He is still in surgery. The process of inserting the new kidney into the recipient is much more complicating than its removal. Dr. Sarif will come out to speak with you as soon as the surgery is complete. I am sure your son will be fine."

"Thank you," Mom replied.

"Yes, thank you very much," I added.

We sat for a few more hours. Aimlessly, I thumbed through magazines, not really reading them. Mom just gazed from wall to wall, wringing her hands in her lap. I glanced at my watch, and when I looked up again, the door had opened. Dr. Sarif was accompanied by his assistant. They both wore the same green scrubs, and both looked weary.

Dr. Sarif spoke first. "Well, it was a very long surgery."

I noticed a faint smile on his face, and the tension in my shoulders began to ease.

"They will both be fine. Your husband did wonderfully well for a man of his age. Your son will have a much longer recuperation process, but we are hopeful."

Mom put her head in her hands and cried happy tears.

"Thank you," Mom said to the nurse.

I wrapped my arms around her in comfort.

"Yes, thank you very much. This has been an exhausting day," I said as they walked out.

In all the years that followed this moment, my mother would devote herself to her son—making his life as normal, fulfilled, and comfortable as possible.

PART II

CHAPTER 10

It was March 1994. Philip had been gone five years. Mom still had her good days and her bad, ebbing and flowing like a cresting wave. We searched for some way of mitigating the sorrow that gripped her. She was functioning on her own now, eating and sleeping better. She tried so hard not to show us her tears, but we knew they were a daily part of her life.

It had taken a few years before I felt myself, finally breaking free of the paralysis that had seized us all. As I stood in front of my bureau mirror taking several long, deep breaths, I realized my nerves were raw. I could have made excuses or blamed Mark, but the fact was I was pregnant. Just the thought made me feel like heaving.

I brushed my hair one more time and went downstairs to get my coat.

"You ready?" Mark asked, helping me slip one arm into the sleeve?

I didn't answer. I was still in shock. Ten minutes earlier, the home pregnancy test had come back positive.

"Are you feeling sick?" he asked.

I shook my head. "Is that a yes or a no?" he asked.

"Ah … no. I'm fine. Let's get this recital out of the way."

"Okay," he said with his eyebrows raised.

This was totally out of character for me. Normally I loved my girls' school recitals. Fortunately, the recital was over in an hour. On the way home, I opened the car window. It was frigid outside, but I was perspiring.

"Close that window. Are you crazy? It's five degrees outside."

"Sorry," I said, closing the window.

How would I tell him? He wouldn't be happy. We had decided long ago that we would have the two girls and no more. Nicole was already in high school, and at thirty-nine, I felt much too old for this pending motherhood. But on the other hand, I knew I could handle this. I was strong. I had always been the rock of the family. I also hated to show weakness, especially in public. How like my father, I thought to myself.

As we both got cleaned up and dressed for bed, there was an unnerving silence between us. I climbed into bed first, then Mark settled in. He lifted his hand to touch mine.

"What is wrong?" he asked sounding exasperated.

With tears in my eyes, I pushed back the bedcovers and shot upright.

"I'm pregnant."

"You're what?"

"Pregnant," I replied with anger in my voice.

Mark seemed to gulp. "Are you sure?"

"Of course I'm sure."

Mark rose from the bed, walked over to the window, and opened it.

For the next several days the tension in the house was palpable. Blaming Mark seemed like a great plan, but he seemed troubled, and I couldn't bring myself to berate him.

Why was he so upset, I wondered. I was the one who would be carrying this child. I was the one who would have morning sickness, swollen ankles, crankiness, and every other miserable symptom imaginable. He needed to buck up and start pandering to *me*, I thought.

We couldn't understand the reality of the situation. We were using reliable birth control, yet I had evidently fallen into the one percent where there is a chance of ineffectiveness. I once thought that number fictitious. Compounding this pregnancy was the deep sense of guilt I was beginning to feel at the thought of not welcoming my own child. What kind of person was I? I thought I knew the answer. I was a person who loved children. I loved being a mother. My life would not have been complete without the joys of motherhood, so what on earth was wrong with me?

After a visit to my gynecologist confirming what I already knew, I decided to call my parents. Dad answered the phone.

"Hi Dad. It's me," I said.

"Hi Donna. You wanna talk to your mother?" I snickered. Dad, every bit the conversationalist. "I can talk to you first."

"Oh, is everything okay?" he asked.

"I suppose so. I'm just leaving the doctor's office. I'm pregnant."

"Oh, that's good. I'll put your mother on the phone now."

Oh my God, I thought. The tone of his voice hadn't even changed. Then I heard my mother in the background, her voice definitely elevated. He had told her before I could.

"Oh, oh," she shrieked. "This is such wonderful news."

I became painfully quiet.

"What's wrong? Aren't you happy?" she asked.

"Well, I didn't expect it, Mom. I'm old for another pregnancy."

"No you're not. Lots of women are having babies over forty. Some don't even have their first until their well into their forties."

Mom's voice was buoyant, her elation creating an overwhelming guilt in me.

"You will have a boy," she insisted. "I just know it. How blessed you will be to have this special child.

"Special?" I asked. "More special than the girls?"

"No, just special in a different way. There is always a purpose under heaven."

I wasn't sure what the purpose would have been for God to have taken her only son, and I'm not sure she really believed what she was saying, but I let her ramble on in sheer delight. When I thought I couldn't take another minute of her bliss, I said, "Okay Mom, I gotta go now."

"All right, honey. I love you."

"I love you too, Mom."

Since Philip had passed, not a day went by without Mom telling me she loved me. She once told me that she hadn't felt she told Philip enough, but I assured her that he knew it in all that she did. There was no escaping the love my mother had for my brother and me. Her eyes told the story. They were her heart and soul.

My mind raced as I was driving home, but I had come to one conclusion; for my mother we had indeed found the "instrument of hope."

Several weeks later, my obstetrician called to discuss my having an amniocentesis.

"Just a precaution," he said. We need to rule out any complications with the child that could arise from your advanced age. The rate for Down syndrome and other disorders jumps significantly if the mother is over thirty-five."

"Oh wonderful," I replied.

"Excuse me," he said.

"Oh, just ignore me. Go ahead and book the appointment for your first available. I don't want to wait in anticipation. It will consume me. I can't take much more of this."

The following month, as I was lying on a cold table, glaring at Mark, the doctor approached the table.

"Are you ready?"

"Not really. Do I have a choice?"

He smiled, turned, and grabbed something from the nurse. It was a needle. A gigantic needle. A needle that looked more fitted for a cow's udder.

"Oh my God. Aren't you going to give me a Novocain? That thing is huge."

"The Novocain will hurt more than the needle," he replied. I am inserting it now."

"Do not give me a play by play," I snapped back.

When it was over, Mark lifted me gently off the table, and we drove home in silence. Humbled, he tried to minimize the misplaced rage I felt when I looked at him. Avoiding conversation seemed to quell the anger.

Our lives were anything but tranquil in the ensuing weeks. Nicole was still moody, speaking only when spoken to, and Mark at this point had become increasingly quiet. Kimmy, at only eight, just went on with her elementary life and all the thrills it offered. She hadn't formulated any real opinion about the baby, other than the fact that there would be some crying in the house. And I just existed in a haze, still not coming to grip with reality.

The phone call came early in the morning as I was getting ready to go to work. I worked as an account executive traveling from store to store within Massachusetts. On this particular morning, I just couldn't get myself acclimated, and at nine o'clock, the telephone wakened me out of my trance.

"Hello," I said.

"Hello, Donna. This is Dr. Carlson. I am calling to inform you of your amnio results."

"Yes."

"I am pleased to tell you that your son appears to be healthy," he said with enthusiasm in his voice.

I paused at the kitchen door, gripping the handle to steady myself. "Thank you. That is very good news."

"Good-bye Donna. I'll see you in four weeks."

My *son*, he had said. My God. She was right. I reached for a glass of water to steady my nerves, then went back and lifted the receiver. The telephone rang. Dad answered it on the first ring.

"Hi, Dad."

"We've been waiting for your call. We're your parents. We worry, although your mother is calmer than I have seen her in five years." He paused. "She has described to me in detail what your son will look like."

"She did? I never told her it was a boy."

"Well, is it?"

"Yes."

"I could draw you a picture after listening to her describe him in detail for the last few days," he said, laughing.

"No," I said incredulously.

"You should see your mother's face. She glows."

"Well, I'm glad someone's glowing," I replied.

And then he put the divine messenger on the phone.

As a little girl, I had watched Nana Maria and Mom spin their magic. They were both incredibly superstitious, and both firmly ensconced in their Catholic faith. How they reconciled the dichotomy was unclear, but they did. I'm sure they had no idea how very pagan their ritual was. They believed that by integrating oil and water, you could watch the "eye" develop. If it did, then you were said to have the "*mallochio*," or evil eye. If it didn't, Nana would still watch to see how the oil and water mixed. She would then interpret the contents of the bowl like a prophecy. I remember watching as they would pray in Italian over the small bowl, stirring and stirring, as if it were a witch's cauldron. If it was determined that an evil eye had been cast on the house, Nana would take the concoction and throw it out the door, or "cast it out." When I was old enough to understand the pure absurdity of it all, I would shake my head and roll my eyes. Nana Maria was the master of this ritual. Mom was merely an observer. However, after Nana passed away, only three months prior to Philip's passing, Mom had assumed the role quite seriously. At this point, I was beginning to question the absurdity of this ceremony, which had been brought to America from the "old country."

I spent the last month of my pregnancy in the hospital. I had developed preeclampsia, and I was confined to bed rest. Every day my blood was checked, my vital signs taken, and my son's heart rate monitored. I wasn't allowed to stand, and was bathed in bed. I stayed calm and accepted that I would be here for the eight weeks to term. During this time, a special bond developed between my son and me. I cradled my belly and grasped his hand when he punched it, and for his sake my every thought was on my ability to make it to term.

That wouldn't be. Toward the latter part of October, I began to gain water weight at an alarming rate, and on this particular fall morning, with the leaves a vibrant red outside my window, Dr. Carlson entered my room. Mark had dropped by on his way to work. He never missed a day. On this morning, his timing could not have been more perfect.

"How are you feeling today, Donna?"

"I feel fine. I've always felt fine."

"Well, unfortunately you are not fine. Your kidneys are struggling with this pregnancy, and your blood pressure is becoming difficult to control."

A lump developed in my throat, and as if the baby knew, my belly catapulted.

"We need to take the baby as soon as possible, preferably tomorrow."

"Absolutely not. No, not tomorrow. Tomorrow is Halloween."

Dr. Carlson looked baffled. "Okay, how about Friday, November 4.

"No!" I shrieked.

Dr. Carlson was beginning to get annoyed. "Is there some reason these dates are unsuitable?" he asked.

I was beginning to quiver when Mark intervened.

"Could I speak to you in the hallway, Dr. Carlson?"

Mark approached the door, and the doctor followed with a skeptical look on his face.

They closed the door gingerly behind them and spoke in hushed tones. I could barely hear what was being discussed.

"I'm sorry this is so complicated, Dr. Carlson, but Donna's brother passed away on Halloween exactly five years ago, and he was buried on November 4. You could not have picked two more inappropriate dates. Surely you understand that we would not want to commemorate a death with a birth."

"Of course I understand. I am so sorry I chose those dates. Very strange," he said as he opened the door to go back into the room.

"Donna, I am sorry. Please try to stay calm. We will take the baby on November 3. Is that okay?"

"Yes, thank you," I said, my eyes blurred with tears. My breathing slowed at last, and my racing pulse with it.

Doctor Carlson closed the door behind him, and Mark came closer to the bed. "Are you crying?" he asked." "Everything's okay now."

I sniffled and looked up at him. " I find myself straining to remember everything about him. I can no longer hear his voice. Little by little his features are vanishing before my eyes. My heart still aches."

Mark stroked my hair, and smiled a smile that went straight to his heart.

Kyle was born by cesarean section at noontime on November 3, 1994. It would prove to be my worst delivery. Kyle was six weeks early and had difficulty breathing. As he was being whisked off to the Neonatal Intensive Care Unit, I was hurried to the Adult Intensive Care Unit. My blood pressure was erratically high, and it would be twenty-four hours before they were able to stabilize me. On the following day, a nurse wheeled me into see the baby. I was not prepared. Mark had spent the day before alternating between both intensive care units, but he never told me what I would encounter when I saw Kyle. He insisted that Kyle was fine.

Kyle looked like a small chicken, skinny and long. He was only five pounds, but he was actually the largest baby in the unit. An oxygen mask was taped on his face, scrunching his nose and eyes into his forehead. He had probes and tubes all over him. I felt faint, and was happy to be in a wheelchair.

"Oh God," I said.

"Now now," the nurse said.

"He's actually doing great. He just looks bad with the mask and tubes."

"Really?"

"Absolutely. I'll get his nurse so you can speak to her."

As we were waiting for the nurse, Kyle let out a scream, and I was suddenly startled out of my pensive immobility. Kyle's nurse approached with a smile on her face.

"Hi, Donna. It's good to see you feeling better. I heard you had a pretty bad day yesterday."

"Yes. How is Kyle?"

"Well, you just heard him. He's doing fine, and we are hopeful that he will be able to eat tomorrow. We're giving him fluids intravenously now, but once we've determined his breathing is stable, you can try feeding him."

"Feed him? I'm scared to hold him."

"Oh no, don't be silly. He won't break. Here," she said as she lifted Kyle tenderly from his isolate.

The guilt I had carried for many months melted away as I held my son. I fell in love with him instantly. The baby's eyes, a light hazel, looked up at me from long brown lashes.

I looked down at him and sniffed the scent of newborn skin. For a long minute I held him against my chest.

"Hello, Chickie."

Chickie was my pet name for my girls, and now my son would wear it well—scawny legs and all. As I peered down at his skinny little face and stroked his head, I saw something in his eyes. I just wasn't sure what it was.

Kyle had beaten the odds. Immediately after Dr. Carlson lifted Kyle from my womb, he began the process of tying my fallopian tubes. We all agreed that my body would not tolerate another pregnancy should it happen. As he was locating the tubes to tie, he found only one tube intact. This meant that I became pregnant with one functioning tube and potent birth control. The odds of that happening were half of one percent.

The baby made remarkable progress and came home with me on the fourth day. The first few weeks he was bitterly thin, but he fed well, and at three weeks, he had gained three pounds. Now instead of a little chicken face, his round pink cheeks were ready to be squeezed. My mother was in place and ready for that first squeeze.

"Look at him. He is beautiful. He looks like me."

It was funny—he did. He had Mom's light hair, light skin, and eyes. But what surprised me even more was that Mom didn't comment on who Kyle really looked like. She had to see it. I finally had.

As we watched Mom interact with Kyle, we noticed the happiness that was once on her face was there again. When she looked down at his little face, the intensity of the love could be felt as well as seen. It emanated from her toes to the top of her head. While she was in his presence she was distracted from her sad thoughts, if only for the moment.

Kyle grew into a happy, bouncy toddler, but some nights even after going to bed laughing, we would hear a blood curdling shriek. His eyes would be closed, and the shrieking would never waken him. The doctors described these episodes as "night terrors." I was told they would scare me more than Kyle, but I didn't believe that. How could the doctors know how he felt during an episode?

The sky was cloudless and the sun was high on this warm May day. I was driving my daughter Kimmy to a friend's birthday party. Kimmy was in the passenger seat, and Kyle was strapped into a car seat in the back. I had the radio on a soft rock station, when Kyle began to speak.

"Mommy, I had a dream last night."

"You did. What was it about?"

"I had a hose down my throat, and I was trying to talk to you, but I couldn't."

"A hose," I asked, my insides turning. "What kind of hose?"

"Like the hose Daddy uses to wash the car, but it wasn't green. It didn't have any color."

I felt the blood draining from my face. I began to shake uncontrollably.

"Mom, are you okay?" Kimmy asked.

I couldn't speak or handle the steering wheel, so I pulled the car off the road.

Kyles mouth quivered slightly.

"Mommy, did I say something wrong?"

"No honey," I replied.

"Mom, what was that all about?" Kimmy whispered.

I couldn't even reply.

"Mom," she said.

"Let me just sit for a minute. I'll tell you when I pick you up later."

When my blood redistributed, I continued driving with an unpleasant flutter in the pit of my stomach. I looked into the rearview mirror at this angelic four-year-old child smiling back at me. I tried to convince myself that what I heard was different from what he said, but when Kimmy returned home, she confirmed Kyle's words.

"I know it was a weird dream, Mom, but why did you get so upset? You really looked like you had seen a ghost."

"Quite literally," I said.

"What?" she asked.

"Kimmy, I'm sure I've never told you about Uncle Philip's last moments, because you were only three years old and wouldn't have understood at the time. On the evening your uncle died, I stood over him in the emergency room urging him to fight and live. He looked up at me with those eyes, those beautiful but sad green eyes. He wanted to tell me something. You could see him try to talk, but he had a ventilator tube down his throat and couldn't."

"What's a ventilator tube?"

"A tube to help him breathe."

"Oh."

"Do you understand now?" I asked.

"Yes, Mom. That is very weird."

"Yes, very much so," I confirmed.

"Hey Mom, remember about a year or two ago when Kyle was in the living room and you were dusting that picture of Uncle Phil?"

"That was weird too. Do you remember what he said?"

"Vaguely, I wasn't paying much attention."

"He pointed to the picture and just said, 'Hi, Uncle Philip.' Don't you remember you kinda looked over at me and asked me if I had ever told him who the man in the picture was?"

I didn't have to think long to remember. My mouth gaped as my eyes swelled.

"Yes, I do remember. Later, when Dad and Nicole came home, I asked them if they had pointed him out also, and they hadn't. Then I asked Kyle, 'Kyle honey, how do you know who the man in the picture is?' and he said, 'Oh, I saw him before in my room, Mommy.' I didn't think much of it at first, since what he said seemed like simple childhood imagination, but now...?"

That evening when Mark returned home from work I told him about Kyle's dream.

"I suppose it's a little strange," he said.

"A little?"

"Well, what do you think it means?" he asked.

"I don't know, but I'm going to find out."

Before I had an opportunity to look into these bizarre events, a third and last one occurred. This one was the most difficult to explain. It happened on a frigid winter day. I was busy preparing cookies for my girls when they arrived home from school. Kyle was at the kitchen table having fun drawing with colored pencils. He was smiling and humming a song from the Barney cartoon.

"Mommy come look at what I made for you." With a huge grin, he lifted the paper and handed it to me. I tried to contain my shock and swallow the lump in my throat as I looked at my son's handiwork. I paused for what seemed like several minutes.

"Wow, Kyle. It's terrific," I said. "Did you copy it from a book?"

"No, Mommy," he replied, smiling.

Kyle had always drawn well for a toddler. When other children his age were drawing stick figures, his characters had form. But, the images before me were beyond the realm of possibility. He drew a green frog and Mickey Mouse. The fluidity of the sample drawings gave an overall impression of spontaneity, imagination, enthusiasm, and precision. Anyone would have found it inconceivable for a four-year-old to have such imagination and precise control of detail. I maintained my composure and acted very matter of fact.

"Can you draw some more for me?" I asked.

"Yes, Mommy."

This time I stood over him watching as he began to draw. The toddler emerged again, with drawings not at all unusual for a child his age.

However, the frog and the Mickey Mouse were impossible to dismiss. When Mark and the girls came home that evening, I showed them the drawings.

"So, what do you think now?" I asked. "Do you think this is normal too?"

They all looked at the images, then each other. They were clearly as confused as me.

"I don't know how to explain it," Mark said. "It is just some freaky incident."

"Yes, freaky would be an understatement. I think I have an answer."

"You do?"

"Do you know someone else in my family that is—I mean was—a wonderful artist?"

"Don't be ridiculous," Mark said.

"Why not? I have no other explanation," I replied.

"Donna, there is no such thing as reincarnation."

"And how can you say that with such conviction?"

"I just can. It's ludicrous," Mark replied, shaking his head.

"Is it? Now you sound like my father. Some things cannot be explained. Think back to the dream Kyle had. How could he have possibly known what transpired in Philip's last moments on this planet? Impossible. I never even told the girls, because they were too young at the time. The only people that knew were you, me, and my parents. I don't believe any of us would find any justification for describing that horrific moment to a four-year-old. What I would really like to know is what Philip wanted to tell me? Why did Kyle not finish the dream and tell me what Philip couldn't all those years ago? I still have no resolution, just an eerie feeling up and down my spine and a four-year-old who has no clue as to what he is experiencing."

"Okay, calm down. I'm sure there is a logical explanation."

He touched my shoulder and tried to guide me toward a chair.

"No."

My eyes cut into his face.

"Logic doesn't work here, Mark. You don't believe in reincarnation, but you believe in the teachings of your faith, unproven teachings possibly from fictitious characters."

"I believe in some of what I was taught," he said. "I guess I believe in the underlying message."

"But not the messenger?" I asked acidly.

"Donna, you're getting much too deep with all this. It was just three bizarre incidences."

Nicole gazed down at the drawings in her hand, her eyes drawn together and her lips pursing.

"But Dad, look at these. How?"

"Give me those," and Mark took them away.

"Fine Mark. You're a skeptic, like my father. If it's not tangible, well, is God tangible? Have you touched him or her lately?"

"Now *you're* thinking like your father," Mark said.

"My father? He believes in nothing."

"That's not true," Mark insisted. "He believes in you. He trusts you."

My eyes began to fill.

"I'm not sure what to think at this point. One thing I do know is that Philip was a true believer. He believed in Christianity, reincarnation, and a multitude of other paranormal phenomena."

"Okay, enough," he shouted. "Don't breathe a word of this to your mother. She will take it to another level and regress to a dark time in her life. We don't want her to think Kyle is Philip. That's just unhealthy—for her, and for you."

I turned sharply on my heels and walked away shaking my head. How much clearer did it need to be? It's as clear as the air we breathe.

Chapter 11

The Roman sun seemed warmer and larger than the sun at home. On this May day in 1998, while standing in the Roman Forum, Mom looked up, almost burning her eyes. The sun was hovering over the ruins and appeared as if it would descend upon them. She removed her straw hat from her satchel, crammed it on her head, and pulled it over her eyes, trying to shut the sun out. The intense sun always caused Mom migraines.

The air was different too: pungent and sweet from the garlic toast being distributed from kiosks by young children. Tourists wandered, their faces glowing in amazement, and nuns chatted while strolling arm in arm through St. Peter's Square.

Mom had been planning this trip to Italy for quite some time. She and Dad would spend their fiftieth wedding anniversary in Rome, Venice, Naples, and Florence. The ten-day guided tour was difficult for Mom to endure with her debilitating arthritis and other conditions, but she persevered. Her mind willed her body to perform in ways that amazed even her.

They were part of a group of tourists primarily from the Northeastern United States. Mom and Dad were the troupe elders. Mostly Italian-Americans, the tour members shared stories of their childhoods and their families. There was a common thread that stitched these strangers together like a family quilt. They shared their recipes and their lives. Mom was the group psychologist, offering advice on raising kids, reinventing marriage, and everything in between. Dad shadowed behind, smirking at her wisdom but eternally grateful for her frivolity. It had been four years since Kyle's birth, and the improvement in her spirit was evident. Her eyes sparkled again, and her facial muscles were more flaccid. The hearty laugh that was so integral to her being had also returned.

The air remained thick and heavy with humidity on what promised to be yet another sultry day under a lingering high pressure system. By late afternoon, the sun was not as blinding, as it was hiding behind the clouds. This was the third day of the tour, and one of the stops would be St. Peter's Basilica. Mom and Dad were looking forward to this day.

They entered the magnificent church walking several steps behind the group. Some of the younger folk kept turning back to check on them.

"Are you two okay?" John Monti asked.

John and his wife, Irene, were from New Jersey.

"Sure, we're fine," Dad replied. "Don't worry about us."

But they did. Just four days before, these people were alien to each other, but now they had become one family, connected on a cultural plain.

"What nice people," Mom said.

"Yep," Dad replied.

The church was bustling with people of many diverse nationalities, all converging upon this most magnificent structure. Some tourists, not aware of the Vatican's strict rules regarding attire, were turned away at the entrance, but

Mom and Dad had been advised of the no shorts or bare shoulders rule. They both wore sneakers, lightly colored slacks, short sleeved shirts, and hats to temper the sun. Dad carried the camera, and Mom made him snap away whenever and wherever it was permitted.

The church was gargantuan, but its peaceful presence wrapped itself soothingly around Mom as she explored. Knowing it was impossible to see in its entirety in the amount of time allowed, Mom explored at an easy pace with Dad strolling closely behind. She was almost mesmerized by the lavish mosaics, but her breath was stolen and her heart felt vacuous when she encountered Michelangelo's *Pieta*. Heavy tears welled up in Mom's eyes as the vision of Mary, holding Jesus when he was removed from the cross, stood before her. As she was wiping her eyes, she felt someone tap her right shoulder. She snapped her head back quickly toward Dad, who stood behind her. Her mouth was open ready to speak, but Dad spoke first.

"What's wrong?" he asked.

"Did you just tap my shoulder?"

"No, why?"

"Are you sure?"

"Of course I'm sure."

Suddenly a fierce sadness sliced through her like a razor. She felt the cut deep in her soul, and choked on a breath.

"Connie, are you okay?" Dad asked.

"Yes, I'm fine," she said quietly. She lowered her head. *Why is it always my right shoulder?* she wondered. Changing her direction suddenly, as if in a trance, she remembered her childhood.

The whole thing seemed like a horrible dream, too absurd to have actually occurred. But in that split second of confused unreality, Connie realized she was wide awake. But the tap. Who had tapped her shoulder? Frantically searching for her father, and hoping that the lady had been a figment of her imagination, Connie ran toward the back bedroom.

"Papa. Papa!"

Eyes widened in confusion, fighting back tears, she burst through her parents' bedroom door. Orazio's dreams were interrupted by the squeaking of the door. He sat straight up and shot a glance at the clock. Two o'clock.

"Concetta. What's wrong?"

Connie looked up at the heap of covers next to Orazio. She pulled them off and found Maria still sound asleep.

"Oh Papa," she cried. "There's a lady in my room. I thought it was Mama, but Mama is here."

"What lady?" he asked.

Tugging at his arm, Connie prodded her father into the hallway and into her bedroom. They turned on the light. Orazio looked around the room and shook his head.

"Whatever are you talking about child? There's no one here."

"Papa, I am not a child. I'm twelve years old, and I tell you I saw her at the foot of my bed. It was dark, but I felt someone touch my shoulder, and when I sat up, she was hovering over me ."

"Who?" Orazio said.

"I don't know who she was. She wore a long, dark dress. Her veiled head was bowed, so I couldn't see her face.

Papa raised his eyebrows. "Concetta, there's no one here.

"No, Papa. I saw the lady."

Orazio took his daughter's hand in his and guided her back to bed, convinced that the whole affair had been a dream. He turned out the light.

"It is time to go back to sleep."

"But Papa!"

"Sleep now. I am just down the hall. I will hear if someone passes my room to get to yours. Sleep."

Connie could not. The terror that shook her held her eyes open until four o'clock, when finally sleep overcame her. The next day, Connie explained the story to Maria, who did not doubt her daughter.

"I will sleep in your room tonight."

"Oh Mama, thank you." Maria gave a weak smile. That day at the store, Maria and Orazio spoke with growing concern several times about Connie's claim to have seen a lady in black. John, the undertaker's son, overheard the conversation. He approached the stock room.

"Orazio," he interrupted.

"Yes."

"Excuse me, but I heard you and Maria talking about a lady in black. That woman may be Anna."

"Anna, who's Anna?" Orazio asked.

"Orazio, where do you live?"

"We live at 52 Wall St."

"That's it!"

Orazio stammered. "That's what?"

"The address of the lady in black."

Orazio removed his apron and motioned John into the back room. "Okay, John. What's this all about?"

"Orazio, I remember about twenty years ago when I was a small child—oh, it must have been around 1906—my father waked a baby in his funeral home. I remember seeing the tiny casket being rolled in the back door, and I asked my father if it was for a doll. It was so small. He didn't answer, but closed the door behind him, flipping the lock. They had left the casket closed for the wake because the mother couldn't bear to see the child in it. Many years later, it was my mother who told me the story of the baby that had died. Died at 52 Wall Street.

Orazio stood and cocked his head toward John. "And so, what does that mean?"

"The baby's mother was named Anna. My father never forgot the anguish in Anna's eyes as he lowered the casket into the ground. Later, after the funeral, a small group gathered at Anna's mother's home. Anna lived two doors down from her mother. During the gathering, Anna's mother noticed her daughter missing and asked her son-in-law to go find her. He found her. Two doors down. She had hanged herself in her bedroom, next to the baby's crib. The baby was a boy. Joseph Novia was his name. They called him Joey. He was two years old, and no one ever determined how he died."

Orazio had paled, bewilderment contorting his face.

"Could it be?" he asked Maria, who had walked in on the conversation. Maria folded her arms, and with a defiant grin said, "I'll see tonight."

Maria had a strong constitution. She didn't fright easily, so the task before her was not as daunting as others might have imagined. Twilight came at once, as it often did after a long, hard day at the store. Maria was fatigued, and the surrender was immediate. The house was quiet as the clock struck two. Maria opened an eye. She felt a breeze and noticed the window was open.

"I thought I closed that," she said. "Hmm." She felt her throat tighten. Shuffling back to bed, she readjusted herself back under the covers. She tossed and turned until the clock struck three. A fading light was casting long shadows across the room. Then she felt something—a powerful presence in the room. She sat up and looked over at the far corner of the room near the open window.

There she was, hovering near the window. Shrouded in black. Maria thought her eyes were playing tricks on her, that what she was seeing was nothing more than a beam of moonlight playing on the blanket over the bed. But the apparition persisted, "looking sadly at me," said Maria. She went to the window, but the night was so black, there was no moonlight. By now Maria gave herself a sign of the cross on her forehead and fled the room at once. Orazio and Maria returned to the room, but the lady was gone.

The following night, Orazio slept in the room. The lady didn't appear. At precisely two o'clock on the third night, the woman appeared again, a third time, to Maria. Maria was not touched by the lady, and everyone wondered why only Connie had been tapped on the shoulder. Very soon after, the Savacas moved to 77 Wall St.

"Connie," A woman's voice said. She looked around and saw Irene Monti trying to get her attention. Mom walked in Irene's direction. Mom had grown quite fond of Irene in a short time. Irene was only a few years younger but much more spry.

"Connie, did you see the *Pieta*? Isn't it magnificent?"

"Yes, it's lovely," Mom replied in a whisper. She lowered her eyes.

Irene looked at Dad questioning Mom's change in mood. Dad just smiled back.

Since meeting Mom, Irene had sensed anguish in her soul. Behind her boisterous laughter, she was a woman tormented. Now, with Mom's sudden change in demeanor, Irene knew her instincts were correct. What could have been so utterly disruptive to her in the Basilica? *Oh,* Irene remembered. *Michelangelo's* Pieta. *But why?* she wondered.

The remainder of the trip was equally insightful as Mom learned about the culture seeded in her being, but each day she found it more and more difficult to keep up. She had wanted to come to Italy for as long as she could remember and would not let her health spoil her dream. She thought of her parents. Sadly, Maria and Orazio were never able to return to their homeland for a visit or even a funeral. They never were able to reclaim their lost assets.

Orazio stood on the dock and watched as the wooden lobster traps were being stacked along the rails. Delivery wagons were lined up and loading barrels of fish and big blocks of ice into the shacks, where fresh fish was weighed, cleaned, and sold. Orazio was lost in deep thought when Gianni turned to him.

"I wish you luck, Orazio," he said in Italian.

"Thank you," Orazio replied.

Gianni offered his hand, and they said good-bye. They had been doing business together for over thirty years, but today would be Orazio's last day on the dock. The store was gone. Maria's illness had devoured all his savings. In the early 1950s, Maria was diagnosed with tuberculosis. Her recuperation period would be long and arduous, but her confinement could be cut dramatically if she were admitted into a private hospital rather than a public one.

Then in 1959, the West End fell to the bulldozers. For the middle-class tastes of city planners and politicians, the West End was considered too crowded and un-American. Slowly, the West End imploded, replaced by high-rises, expensive apartment buildings, and new wings of Massachusetts General Hospital. Residents were forced out into the streets. The Urban Renewal Project tore apart the fabric of this tight-knit Italian-American community. For Orazio and Maria, the days of opera, dancing, and fine furs were gone. They settled into a small tenement building in the North End of Boston, another exclusively Italian neighborhood. Their apartment had one bedroom, a tiny living room, and a kitchen. The bathroom was outside the unit, in a cold, drafty common hallway. There was no tub or shower. The home they lived in previously was also in a tenement building, but it had two large bedrooms, a dining and living room, a kitchen, and an indoor bathroom. The rent at the new apartment was only ten dollars a month, considerably less than their former home. Orazio retired from the grocery business, partly because he had debilitating arthritis that was claiming his body, and also because he no longer had the resources necessary to start over. Maria was well now, and she took a full-time job as a seamstress. They made ends meet, and they never complained about their financial and social decline. Much of the daily social life took place on the street; therefore, watching this social life from the window—elbows on a pillow—was a common spare-time activity in the West End, and particularly so with the elderly. Many were still without cars and had little money. Not understanding much of what they observed, they existed in a tiny speck of the universe and never ventured outside their safety zone. Most had been here for at least thirty years, and they still didn't understand this country called "America."

The Alitalia 737 raised its wings higher into the clouds, and Mom watched the ruins of Rome gradually fade from sight. She smiled and sighed. Soon she felt the plane level off and glanced over at Dad, who seemed unusually pale. He complained about being light headed, and before Mom could reach him, he fainted. Mom became frantic, thinking he had died. When a doctor on board finally brought him back to consciousness, Mom looked down at him and said, "Don't you ever do that to me again." She began to cry.

"I'll try not to," he said with a blanched smile.

Chapter 12

The news wasn't good. Dad could feel the hair rising on his forearms, and he rubbed them uneasily. He sat in a sparsely furnished examining room waiting for the doctor to arrive. He had never met this doctor, whom his internist had referred. He tried to remain optimistic, but the phone call had seemed dire.

Doctor Newman had called the week before with the blood results. Dad's creatinine levels were severely elevated. When Dad asked what that meant, he was told it meant his remaining kidney was not functioning to capacity. He had gulped when the doctor said the word "remaining." This would explain why he had edema and was frequently tired, the doctor said. Dad asked if this meant his kidney was failing, and Dr. Newman replied in the affirmative. He then recommended that Dad see a nephrologist, a doctor who specializes in conditions of the kidneys, to assess his individual situation.

A week later, he sat hoping that the doctor was wrong. Dad knew only too well what life was like living on a machine. You have virtually no life. He watched his son endure the ordeal for three years. He remembered picking Philip up from his treatment three days a week. He dreaded walking into the room, blaring away with machines oozing in red blood. He felt as though he were entering the room of the living dead. The patients were gaunt and pale. Most had difficulty walking out, while some were on stretchers. The thought of his life ending this way made him cringe. Then he thought, *My poor son. This must be how he felt too, and he was only thirty-seven. I'm eighty-three. I have no cause to complain.* He paused, looked out the window, and thought, *Oh heck, I'm just jumping to all kinds of conclusions.* A knot formed in his throat. *This is most likely just a warning. I'll watch my diet and keep taking my vitamins. They haven't let me down yet.* Dad had always been diligent about eating the right foods, taking his vitamins, and staying in shape.

Then he heard footsteps in the hallway, and the doctor lifting his chart from the sleeve in the door. When the door opened, a very young man walked in. "Hello, Mr. Tullio. I am Dr. Johnson." He extended his hand. Dad took his hand and gave it a firm shake.

"Hi, Doc." It's nice to meet you. "So, why am I here?"

"Frank, you are in late stage renal failure."

"I'm what?"

"Your kidney is not excreting waste from your body, and since you are too old for a transplant, you will need to have dialysis."

"When?" Dad asked, his mouth frozen.

"As soon as possible. We do not want you to get so sick that you start having other complications, like congestive heart failure and a variety of other problems." He glanced at Dad's chart again. "I understand you donated a kidney to your son fourteen years ago?'

"Yes."

"And how is he doing?"

"We lost him a few years after the transplant."

"I'm sorry," Dr. Johnson replied.

Dad hesitated, then said, "Is that the reason I am here, because I gave my son a kidney?"

"I can't say for certain. As some people advance in age, their kidneys start to fail. However, most people can go a lifetime with no kidney problems whatsoever. We don't know all the causes. Diabetes is a major contributor to kidney disease, but you do not have that."

"My son did," Dad said.

"Oh. I'm not sure what caused your current condition," the doctor replied.

"Well, I remember when I was being screened for the donation. The doctor in charge of my pre-surgical testing told me that donating a kidney could cost me fifteen years off my lifespan. The other doctors told me that there were no adverse side effects to donating the kidney. Who was I to believe at the time? Obviously the doctor in charge of my testing was accurate," Dad said defiantly.

"Well, I'm not sure I agree with that, and even if that were true, would it have changed your decision to give your son life?"

"No," Dad replied.

"Well, then it's a moot point."

"Do you want to think this over? I realize it is a lot to absorb."

"Yes." Dad looked toward the window, the bright sun flashed in his eyes, and he blinked. "My son suffered miserably while on dialysis." He looked back toward the doctor. "God, I never thought I would have to look at another one of those death rooms again. Maybe I just won't do it."

"If you don't, Frank, you will die in the very near future. You know, everyone tolerates dialysis differently. You won't necessarily have the same reaction to the treatment. Your body may tolerate it better than your son's did."

"Hmm," Dad murmured. He extended his hand. "Thanks, Doc."

"Good luck, Frank."

Dad dressed slowly, his mind far away. His first thought was, how would he ever tell Mom? He drove home recklessly, something he had never done since Mike Hardy drove his fiancée into a tree. He thought about Mike for a quick moment. Dad hardly ever had a hard drink after that accident, sticking with an occasional beer or wine. He had led a very safe life to this point.

When Dad arrived home he walked quietly into the kitchen. Mom was resting, but she heard his footsteps and came into the kitchen. She fluffed her hair with her fingers and straightened her housecoat.

"How did it turn out, Frank?" she asked.

"Not good."

"What do you mean?"

"They want me to go on dialysis."

"No, no, no!" Mom screamed.

"Connie, stop screaming. You're gonna have a stroke." But she continued, her screams eventually breaking down into sobs.

"I don't think I wanna go through with this. I remember what Philip went through."

Mom's head came out of her hands and she craned her neck toward Dad. Her eyes opened wider.

"What do you mean? You must have the dialysis."

"It's no life, Connie. I wanna leave this world strong, not weak and withered away."

"Please, Frank. You can't leave me. I cannot go through another death in this family. Please."

The sobbing ensued. He lifted her gently and set her back to bed. Then, sitting on the edge, he placed his hand over hers and said, "Hush now. It'll be fine. Don't worry." When she cried herself back to sleep, he called me. I was expecting the phone call.

"Hi, Dad. How did the appointment go?"

"They want me on dialysis as soon as possible," he said matter-of-factly.

"God, Dad. Are they sure?"

"A hundred percent."

"When will you start?"

"I'm not sure I will start."

"What do you mean? You have to start."

"I don't want to end up like your brother. Do you remember how awful it was watching him? Do you want to put us all through that again?"

"No, Dad, but Mom will die if something happens to you. She will just fall over and not get back up. She really never recovered from losing Philip, but to lose you too?"

"I know. Your mother is the only reason I'm even considering it. The doctor said I might tolerate the treatment better than Philip did."

"Maybe he's right. I think you need to at least try. If you encounter the same problems Philip did, then you can stop. But at least give it a try, Dad, please."

I heard silence, and then a heavy sigh. He was reconsidering.

"You know, many years ago when I was just a little boy, a doctor wanted to remove my right hand. Did I ever tell you that story?"

"Yes Dad. You did."

"Well, my mother didn't know much being an immigrant, but she knew enough to look at my hand and say no, it's fine. Imagine what my life would have been like without my hand. Doctors make mistakes."

"Not this time, Dad."

"Fine. I hope you're right. I'll go tell your mother now. She's shaking in her sleep. I'll wake her, and then maybe she'll settle down." He went back to the bed and shook her shoulder lightly.

"Connie, wake up."

She woke easily, not really in a deep slumber to begin with. She looked up at him, her eyes pleading.

He cradled her in his arms and said, "I'm doing this for you. I know how much you need me. I love you," he added. He hadn't said those words in fifty-seven years.

The following week, the surgeons inserted a shunt into the artery in Dad's arm, and six weeks later he began dialysis. He seemed to do quite well, and insisted on walking out of the hospital on his own.

"I was a sergeant in the army, you know."

***

Dad noticed a crimson glow emanating from beneath Mom's bedroom door. He opened the door slightly and found her kneeling in front of her dresser. The dresser held several photos of Philip at various stages in his life, and next to each photo stood a red votive candle casting a warm glow upon each photo and illuminating Philip's face with a wavering illusion of life. The shrine had occupied her bedroom for fifteen years. Dad still remembered the day Mom set it up. It was the day Sarah had come to the house. Mom was fatigued, running on no sleep and little food, when the doorbell rang. It was Sarah.

"I'll get the door," Dad shouted.

Dad looked through the peephole and saw Sarah standing there alone. He hesitated and thought for a moment about not allowing her in, but then slowly turned the door handle.

"Hello, Frank," Sarah said.

The salutation was not returned, as Dad shot her a look of withering contempt.

"Connie, Sarah's here," he shouted toward Mom's bedroom.

He continued staring at Sarah with a rigid silence, then proceeded toward the back of the house.

Mom sat up in her bed. Not only was she dealing with the grief of losing a child, but she was dealing with the rage. When it came to matters of right and wrong, of loyalty and abandonment, Mom was a fundamentalist. She *always* made her opinion known and rarely backed down from her convictions. She thought about the last time she had seen Sarah, at the funeral a few short weeks ago. Where had the weeks gone, she wondered as she struggled to shift her legs over the side of the bed. Bracing herself against the bed, she tried valiantly to compose herself, but the shaking continued. Mom heard footsteps approach.

"You can deal with her," Dad said. "I'm going upstairs. I can't even stand to look at her," and he blundered off.

Mom shook her head numbly, and with shaking steps, she walked toward the living room. Her eyes bore down on Sarah. Sarah could see the accusation in Mom's eyes, but before she could speak, Mom's rage was unleashed.

"There are certain things a woman owes her husband in time of need. You left him all alone to deal with his illness. We tried to give him some peace and happiness, but he needed you. How could you abandon him?"

"I loved Philip," Sarah replied.

"Love? I haven't seen you shed a tear!"

It was true, she hadn't cried in front of Mom.

"Connie, there's nothing I can say to make you feel better."

Mom slumped in a chair.

"No one can make me feel better. I will never feel better! Do you even wish that he were still alive?" There was an unbridled fury in Mom's eyes. "You killed my son—slowly," she said, her voice growing louder.

"Connie, he was sick."

"Yes, he was, but you made his illness worsen more quickly. You gave him the worst pain imaginable, emotional pain. How could you do that to a sick man? He died unhappy."

Mom's sobbing became intense. "Get out of my house!" she ordered.

Mom braced herself to stand, her eyes darting from Sarah to the door. Sarah turned and quietly closed the door behind her. When Dad heard the door close, he came back downstairs to find Mom lumbering toward her bedroom shaking uncontrollably. She willed her legs to reach her bedroom, where she drew the blinds, released her body onto the bed, and for the remainder of the day, left the world behind.

Chapter 13

"Yep, we won that one too."

Dad was boasting after completing our fourth game of whist. I had grown up playing whist instead of bridge. Dad had taught me to play when I was ten years old. By twelve, I was playing competitively at the whist club down on Cape Cod, where we owned a summer house.

"Yeah, you won again," I replied, smiling.

It was New Years Eve 2003. Mark and I had decided to pick up some lobsters and surprise my parents. We rarely spent New Year's Eve with them, but Dad had begun dialysis a few months prior, and Mom was almost completely confined to the bed. Her debilitating spinal conditions caused her severe, chronic pain, and she was becoming increasingly weak. After Philip died, she had also been diagnosed with Addison's disease, an autoimmune disease that causes your adrenal glands to stop producing the hormones you need to survive. It can be the result of trauma, which I believe it was in her case. Concerned with drug interactions, her doctors were averse to prescribing the necessary medication for total pain management. She never complained, but we could easily see the pain in her eyes. It was constant and extreme.

Although Dad seemed to be marching forward and not complaining, we knew the dialysis treatments were very hard on his body. When we would ask how he was feeling, he would say great. But he was slowly beginning to lose weight. His face, now gaunt, was also changing color. The pinkness was gone, replaced by a sallow, gray tinge. His eyes seemed to be sinking to the back of his skull. So many times I would offer to come and clean up a bit—do the heavy cleaning, bathrooms, floors—the hard stuff, but they would decline the offer every time.

"You have your own life and three children," Dad would say. "You don't need to take care of us too."

Mom agreed. "Yes. All I did was take care of my brothers and clean the house when I was young. I suppose there was no choice. Mom had to work in the store all day with Dad, but there were plenty of times I resented it. I always said that I would never do that to my kids. You were not born to be a servant to me," she would say with resolve.

At this time, Mom was seventy-nine, and Dad was eighty-three. They were very independent, always had been, and never wanted to be a burden on me. But this determined independence caused me more worry. There were times I tried to insist, but I never won an argument, and not wanting to upset them, I would let it go.

The evening ended on a happy note—Mom and Dad taking seven of the nine games. Mark and I were happy to oblige. Mark lifted Kyle off the sofa, and we drove home.

"Your parents really enjoyed tonight," Mark said with affection. He loved my parents almost as much as I did.

"Yes, I am so glad we spent the evening with them. They really need to be our primary focus."

"Absolutely."

***

An endless expanse of silvery flakes weaved a frosted tapestry across the windshield. Drifting across it in blinding sheets of white, Nicole gripped the steering wheel hard, and squinted through the windshield wipers.

"Damn snow," she cursed. She hated driving in this damn stuff. She continued on at a snail's pace, but her car slid on a patch of black ice. She tried to straighten it, but was still having difficulty seeing. Up ahead she saw Exit 17, my parents' exit. Her car veered slowly off the highway. She parked in front of the house and walked briskly toward the door, snow streaking her vision as she swiped her hand at evergreen branches bowed down with glazed frost.

Nicole rang the doorbell, her whole body shivering. The door opened.

"Sweetheart, what are you doing out on this miserable night? Get in here. Where are your gloves? Do you young people not wear boots and gloves?" Dad asked.

Dad called both my girls sweetheart. It was endearing, and it always made them feel special.

"I'm fine, Papa. I am on my way to Boston University for a class, and I thought I should stop for a few minutes to see if the weather improves."

"Yes, yes, good idea. Connie," he hollered into the back bedroom. Nicole's here. Go back, Nana's in bed. She's not feeling well, but she'll feel better when she sees you."

Nicole kissed Dad and went to Mom's room at the back of the house.

Mom was struggling to sit up as Nicole entered the room.

"Hi, Nana," Nicole said.

"Hi, honey. I heard you and your grandfather talking. It is a terrible night to be traveling. Listen, I've got a proposition for you. Let's make some food, talk about boys, and you can skip class. Just this once. I'll never tell your mother."

"Oh, Nana, that sounds great. You're the best." She hugged her grandmother, whom she had adored from her first moments on this earth. Mom placed her warm, smooth cheek on Nicole's cheek, something she had always done. How lovingly familiar this felt, Nicole thought, as she snuggled in closer to Mom. They ate and talked for about two hours. Mom was good at giving advice. She was very progressive, not at all old fashioned. She was also not at all inhibited while offering her advice. She would preface her sermons with, "In case your mother didn't tell you this, I will." I think she thought I was more old fashion than she was. Perhaps I was, but I never minded that she took it upon herself to lecture my girls. She loved them as much as she did me and felt it was her duty. I never took issue with what she had told them. It was usually pretty smart stuff.

"Nicole," she said, "someday when you meet the right boy, you'll know it. Make sure he thinks you are the most beautiful person he has ever seen, and make sure he is kind."

"Yes, Nana."

"You know, last week, I looked into the mirror, and I didn't like what looked back. I am old, ugly, and fat, but once I was beautiful."

"Nana, you're still beautiful."

"No, honey. These medicines have made me fat, and the pain has warped my face, but do you know what your grandfather said to me as I was crying in the mirror?"

"No, what?"

"He said, Connie, you are as beautiful to me now as you were the first day I laid my eyes on you in that dance hall." She exhaled loudly, sounding happy.

Nicole's eyes filled, as did Mom's. They had the same exact eyes, so green and lucid you could almost see into their souls.

"Oh, Nana, that's so sweet. I didn't know Papa had it in him."

"Yes, every now and then your Papa can be sweet, but it doesn't happen very often. He's just never been an emotional guy, but he has always loved us all. You know we all need someone to know us as we truly are and love us anyway."

"I know that, Nana."

"Do you?"

Nicole was my first born, and Mom's first granddaughter. Mom took care of Nicole frequently when she was a baby, as I worked as a flight attendant for Eastern Airlines, which meant I was gone sometimes for two or three days at a time. Grandmother and granddaughter bonded very early on.

When it became time for Nicole to leave, Mom watched from the window. A few seconds later, she adjusted her eyes and blinked. What was that? A bird in the winter? It was. It was a cardinal perched on the forsythia bush by the driveway. Her eyes filled with tears. The bird turned and seemed to look at her through the window, then circled around the bush twice and took flight.

Chapter 14

The telephone woke me with a startle. Through the blur I saw the clock: 1:30 AM. I picked up the receiver. It was Dad.

"Your mother has been rushed to the hospital. I woke to go to the bathroom and found her on the kitchen floor. I think she had been there for a long time. She said she kept calling for me, but I didn't hear her.

"Oh God, Dad. Was she conscious when they took her away?"

"Yes."

"Well, that's good," I said.

"Donna, I can't meet you up at the hospital because I had my dialysis today, and I am too weak to go." He spoke quickly. "I have called Diane, since she lives nearby and can get there quicker than you can."

Diane was Mom's niece. Mom's brother Sam was married to a woman who passed away when she was forty-two, leaving her two-year-old daughter, Diane. Because Sam was disabled, Mom and Dad became more like parents than an aunt and uncle. Diane lived in the upstairs apartment in my parents' two-family home. Obviously, they became very attached.

"I will leave immediately, Dad," I responded.

It had been fifteen years since the last time I dashed up this same highway, to the same hospital. I felt immediate dread. Once again, I had no specifics and did not know what to expect when I arrived.

It seemed to take an eternity to get to the hospital. As I walked toward the emergency room, a cacophony of chattering voices behind me, I had a flash of thought, something my mother had once shared with me about coincidences. She believed that the events we dismiss as coincidence aren't. They're related, and if you go back far enough, you'll see the connection. I wondered what insight my mother could offer now. The voices became louder as I followed a corridor so familiar that I can remember the feel of the floor on my feet. God, how I wanted to turn around and run away before it got me. The emergency room hadn't changed. It was still a portrait of bleak fluorescence.

The nurse took my arm and escorted me through the department door and down a hall toward the curtained bays, an orchestra of electronic beeps rising around them. We stopped, and the nurse pulled back the curtain. I saw my mother on a gurney sitting partially up, with no tubes, masks, or wires. My heart began to resume its normal rhythm, my relief heard in an almost silent sigh.

"Thank God," I said to the nurse. "She doesn't look too bad."

"Yes, we've stabilized her. The doctor will be out shortly to speak with you."

"Thank you," I said.

Doctor Sampson approached and introduced herself.

"Your mother has had an Addisonian crisis, but is stabilized."

"An Addisonian crisis"?

"She may have forgotten to take her hydrocortisone, or she didn't take enough, but she was significantly low. We will keep her for a few days just for observation. She is elderly and weak, and I understand your father is not well enough to care for her."

"Yes, he cared for her until recently when he began dialysis. He still tries, but he can't lift her anymore if she falls. He's struggling to take care of himself now, and I'm struggling with them both."

"I know it's very hard for the children of elderly parents. Do you have siblings to help?"

"Well, my brother is gone, but my cousin helps." I nodded my head toward Diane.

"Well, good luck," Dr. Sampson said, and she went on to her next patient.

I breathed a throaty sigh filled with relief. My sense of dread had been totally unfounded this time. With a cautious smile on my face, I walked over to Mom. She was conscious and coherent but pale. There was a profound sadness in her crystal green eyes. I entered the tiny examining room and kissed her cheek. She barely returned the gesture.

"Why so sad?" I asked. "It looks to me like they've stabilized you. Your doctor has assured me that you'll be fine in no time."

"Yes," she replied.

"Did you forget to take your medicine?"

"I'm not sure," she said. "I only remember waking up on the floor."

"Well, not to worry. You will be fine."

Again, no response, just a silent, vacant stare. Diane was standing next to the bed as I sat in the chair at the foot. I began making some small talk, and soon noticed that Diane appeared distracted. As I spoke directly to her, she was glancing over my head, not looking straight at me. Squinting, she appeared to be trying to focus on an object. I turned my head in the same direction but saw nothing unusual. Then she squinted several more times before approaching my chair.

She bent forward and whispered. "I know you are going to think I'm crazy, but Philip is standing ten feet from your left foot. "

My skin crawled, and my breath was taken away. I arched my back and glanced ten feet toward the left. Then I looked up at Diane with my mouth slightly open.

"I can't really describe it in a concrete sense," she said. "I see a formless vision, and I can feel his presence. There is something there." She pointed, whispering so Mom would not hear.

Yes, I thought she was crazy, and with a smirk on my face I stood and walked over to the spot where she claimed this apparition appeared. I walked through and around more than once. I didn't feel a drop in the surrounding temperature or a thickening of the atmosphere. I not only denounced the presence of my brother, but I was quite emphatic and angry. I scoffed at her encounter and signaled my disapproval with a cold, cutting glare. Again, she bent forward and whispered, "I am telling you he is here, and he has come for her."

My annoyance piqued. I could feel the anger flushing my face. Mom was stable, and the prognosis was adequate, if not rosy. My reaction was swift and determined. I wanted to scream at her, but I had to keep my voice to a minimum.

"Yes, you are right about one thing. I think you are crazy. Mom is fine. No one has come for her, especially a ghost—the word scares the hell out of me."

"That is the reason you can't see or feel him," Diane said. "You don't believe."

I thought about the possibility for a second. They say ghosts inhabit disquieting locations. A hospital emergency room seemed a likely location for this occurrence, even more so because Philip had died in this very same emergency room. *No, don't even allow yourself to think like that*, I thought. My God, I wanted to shout, but I couldn't. Mom was watching us quietly but closely, that eerily absent look in her eyes. I stood and approached her bed with an enthusiastic smile.

"Mom you are going to be fine. They will be transferring you to a room shortly."

She smiled faintly.

"I'm going to leave now to get some sleep before I need to get the kids off to school. I will return tomorrow afternoon." I kissed her again and walked away confident that Diane had imagined this vision.

The next day was Tuesday, and I waited for my Nicole to finish her work day. She worked in a local school system, and her day ended at 2:30. She wanted to accompany me up to the hospital to visit Mom. Nicole and I cheerfully entered the room. I could see Mom's eyes brighten a bit when she saw Nicole, but the flash was quickly shadowed. We kissed and hugged. Nicole and Mom snuggled their cheeks together. The gesture brought tears to my eyes, as it always did. We spoke in generalities about the day. Nicole and I did most of the talking, and Mom shook her head occasionally to acknowledge what she had heard. We discussed

Nicole's job, and how mild the weather was for January. We didn't speak about her condition or her return home. I wanted to keep the discussion light. The mind can lead the body into dangerous territory if you allow it to. I knew that a positive attitude was the first step toward recovery, and I had to maneuver Mom's mind delicately. The doctors were optimistic, but she clearly was not.

We tried to summon more reserved smiles from Mom, but the smiles were tainted with a sadness that remained in her eyes. I lowered my eyes and thought about the claim Diane had made the evening before. Diane graduated summa cum laude from a fine Boston University. She was rational, well educated, and not prone to hysteria or theatrics. Why would she have made such a disturbing remark? The outside world escaped me for a moment, until finally I heard my daughters voice. "Mom."

We spent the next two hours by Mom's bedside trying to get her to nibble on her lunch, which was still on her tray almost untouched three hours after it had been delivered.

"You need food for strength, Mom," I said.

"Perhaps just a bit. I'm not hungry," she responded.

"How about some nice body lotion, Nana? I'll rub some on your arms and legs. They look dry."

"Okay, honey. Thank you."

She picked up the small sample size body lotion sitting on the bedside table. The smell of the lotion was as putrid as the hospital room, a wave of sickness and death that sat above us like a smog-infested cloud, creeping into our mouths and causing a gag reflex. When it was time for us to leave, we both kissed Mom and proceeded out with a slight wave. Nicole was walking behind me. Before she closed the door behind her, she looked back one more time. Mom was crying and just staring at her as she walked out.

Everything happened so quickly.

"Ladies, I'm sorry, but I need to leave now. I want to get up the hospital to check on my Mom before the rush hour traffic starts," I said.

"How is she doing?" my friend Linda asked.

"She's doing fine. They will be sending her home soon. It's hard because she is always in such severe pain from her spine degeneration, and with my Dad on dialysis now, I'm worried. I feel like I should take them both home with me. I have the room, but whenever I broach the subject, they get angry. They've been in that house for over sixty years, and they have said that the only way they'll leave it is with a blanket over them. Isn't that horrible?" I asked.

"Yes," they said in unison.

I put my share of the bill on the table, kissed my friends individually, and went to my car.

I drove leisurely north to the hospital. This was another unusually mild day for late January. The sky was blue and cloudless. I removed my coat while driving and opened a window. I felt as worry free as the gentle air that wafted around me.

I sauntered casually into Mom's room with the air still transporting me. I had had a great day at work and a very nice lunch with my friends.

"Hi, Mom," I said. "How are you today? You look good."

"I'm glad you're here," she said almost sternly. "You need to sit here close to me and listen very carefully."

"Okay," I said, puzzled. I leaned closer, ready to listen.

She huffed as if trying to catch a big breath.

"The doctors have said that my veins are collapsing, and they want to put a central line into my chest."

"Oh, that's not unusual, Mom. They do that for precaution in case they need to get some medicines into you quickly."

"Yes, I know, but I do not want it. Do you understand?"

"Yes. I'll tell them they need to find another way to get the medicines into you."

"No, you do not understand," she said. "I want all medications stopped completely. Everything."

I looked at her, confused. Her expression was vacant.

"Well, Mom, you can't do that. I don't think you understand what you're saying. If you stop all your medications you will slowly die," I said, trying to maintain my calm.

I thought that she truly did not understand the ramifications of what she was saying, but she did.

"Please," she said. "Just sit and listen."

I sat reluctantly, the panic rising in my stomach, the vacuum beginning to suck me away again. She straightened her head and looked intently at me. She reached for my hand.

"You must let me go now," she said. "I'm not afraid, because Philip is right next to me. He has been here for a few days now. I am very warm." Her lips were pressed against each other firmly.

I began to shake uncontrollably and could not speak. She was unquestionably in full possession of her senses. She was well oriented to her surroundings and was insistent on Philip's place next to her. I didn't ask her what she meant. I just quivered in disbelief. She continued.

"I have spent many years trying to survive for the sake of everyone: you, your father, your children, but mostly for you. I went on breathing for you, but do you have any idea what every breath felt like? It felt like someone was squeezing my lungs shut. When I went to bed at night, and when I woke the next day, the hands in my chest were slowly squeezing the life right out of me. I have no breath left. I've suffocated. Do you understand?" she asked.

I wept bitterly, surrendering to my fear, heartbreak, and confusion. Slowly, I quieted my sobs just enough to say, "Yes."

"You are the reason I have existed. I think Dad will be fine when I'm gone, but you?"

I couldn't even fathom the answer to that question.

"I have been happy at times, as happy as I could possibly be, but I have also been waiting to be with your brother again, and now he has come for me. This is the end." Her voice trailed off.

"No it isn't," I shot back.

"Yes it is, and now I need you to promise me some things."

She choked for a moment, then swallowed and looked right into my soul. Paralyzed with fear and wracking sobs, I did not interrupt; I simply nodded involuntarily, as if a string were attached to my head. I sat hunched over as she continued.

"I want you to go to Italy for your twenty-fifth wedding anniversary. Don't wait until you're too old to be able to really enjoy it. That trip was one of the best experiences of my life, but it killed me. Promise me you'll go soon."

I stifled a sob and tried to smile. "Okay, Mom. I will."

"Good girl. Now, you need to buy Kyle a dog. You know how your brother loved dogs. I do too. The girls will be gone off to college, and he will be alone. Every boy needs a dog. Dogs have souls, you know." In a breath or two I was able to look up.

"They do?" I asked.

"Yes."

I thought how mundane this was at this heart-wrenching time. What was she thinking? I was trembling with fear and didn't seem to comprehend her words, but they were being imprinted indelibly into the recesses of my mind.

"Tell Daddy that he made me laugh, sometimes, and tell your girls how very proud I am of them. And you. I want you to learn to be a little selfish. Don't always sacrifice everything for the kids. You never do anything for yourself. I don't want you to be like me. It's okay to think of yourself now and then. She paused for a minute.

"Mom," I said. She continued.

"Philip has said to tell Steven to stop crying for him. He wants his son to go on with his life. It's been fifteen years. And…" she paused, "he wants you to forgive Sarah. I have," she said.

"How can I? She deserted him!"

"Did she?" she asked.

"Yes," I replied.

"You must forgive," she almost scolded, glancing sideways as if acknowledging someone. She smiled at no one.

I felt a shiver go down my spine and right out from my feet. Then she paused for one last remark. "For every death a child is born."

I cocked my head sideways and squinted.

Where did that come from? How clichéd, I thought. It made no sense at all. Mom never spoke in clichés. My crying was now causing me to gag, and I felt I was being thrown against a wall of concrete, my head blasting with pain.

"Now kiss me good-bye," she said. "You have to stop crying. You're making me cry, and I don't want you to remember me like this," her voice cracked as our tears mingled.

A sense of being utterly present and also simultaneously far away came over me. I struggled to compose myself, but I couldn't. I touched her cheek with mine and drew in her smell. I hugged and kissed her, and she me, tightly and together for one last time. Then she closed her eyes. Afterward, I remember screaming and remembered running.

Somehow I ended up at the nurses' station. I don't recall how I got there. I vaguely remember asking the nurses to call Mom's personal physician, not the doctor on call that evening. I remember calling my father to come to the hospital immediately, but it was sometime before I composed myself enough to go back into the room and confront the situation. When I finally did, my mother had closed her eyes and stopped speaking.

"Mom, open your eyes," I cried. "Dad's on his way. Please wake up."

She did not open her eyes. She was very still but clearly breathing and still very much with us. I couldn't sit, so I stood by her bed, shaking my head in disbelief. Shortly after, Dad walked into the room.

"What's wrong?" he asked. "It looks like your mother's sleeping peacefully. Your phone call scared me half to death!"

"Dad, she's not sleeping."

I looked into his eyes and saw a flashback. What she had said was so incredibly jarring, that I momentarily blocked it from my mind. But now, how could I tell my father?

"Dad, Mom said good-bye to me tonight. And she told me what to say to you and everyone else. Dad, when she was done, she just closed her eyes."

Dad moved toward Mom's bed and looked down at her. He blinked and closed his eyes briefly. He sat next to Mom's bed, but he couldn't find anything to say.

"Dad, don't you see?" "Philip has let Mom stay with us all these years. Now we have to give her back to him."

Dad's lips quivered, and he pressed them together for a minute.

"Are you sure?" he asked. "It's just so crazy."

"I know it sounds crazy, but I repeated it word for word to you. I barely understand it myself."

Dad looked at me with a puzzled look, and I thought he would question me further, but after a short hesitation, he laid his hand on top of hers, feeling the warmth and the pulse against his fingers, and kissed her cheek lightly. Then he stood, and with his shoulders drooped, his gait slow, and his head bent, he walked out of the room. They never said good-bye.

The next forty-eight hours were a blur. My mind kept replaying images of the good-bye. I was astonished at how brave my mother was. She was meeting death head on, not with fear but with complete acceptance. I always knew my mother had courage. She never let me see her cry for my brother, but my father would tell me about the long, difficult evenings that were now as common as they were when Philip passed.

I spent the majority of the next two days in my mother's hospital room, going home only for a short catnap or a change of clothes. Sleeping was futile with the weight of her farewell on my chest, but I tried to close my eyes from 1:00 a.m. to 5:00 a.m. The doctors said it would be about a week or two for her body to break down to the point of collapse. Mom's body was dependent on the hydrocortisone that supplied what her adrenal glands did not. Without that hormone, her heart would eventually stop.

It was 5:30 a.m. on Thursday when I finally dragged myself out of bed. The early morning air was warm for late January, albeit overcast. I threw on my khaki pants and a heavy black sweater and tossed my hair up in a clip, rushing out of the house without putting on any makeup. I drove up the highway in a fog, guided not by sight but by a hand. At 5:45 I stepped off the elevator and into her room. She was very agitated and appeared uncomfortable. Her eyes were still closed, but fluttering as she thrashed and moaned. I began to feel panicked and confused. Was she in pain, or was she struggling to come back? What if she had changed her mind about her decision to leave? Could we even go back to her physical state prior to the withdrawal of medicine, or had permanent damage been done? These questions were spinning in my mind, and answers did not exist. At this point, I stood next to her bed pleading, "Please, please open your eyes, Mom, and tell me what is wrong."

No response. A moment later, I rang the red call button attached to her pillow and called for the nurse. She arrived quickly.

"Why is she thrashing this way?" I asked, my voice bordering on hysteria. "Why does she seem so uncomfortable?"

"I don't know, but I'll make some calls," she replied as she tucked Mom into her bed snuggly. She called my mother's personal physician, and I waited. When it became intolerable to watch, I stepped out into the corridor. I felt a responsibility to console her, but watching this nightmare unfold was more than my body could take. Dr. Spitzer arrived about an hour later. I was quickly unraveling, questioning myself. Should I have fought her final request to stop the medication? I voiced my concerns, including those about my decision. He replied, "Donna, I arrived here late last evening after you had gone home. Although she was definitely unresponsive when I first arrived, I commanded her to open her eyes several times, and finally she did."

"Really?" I said. "That's hard to believe. I tried all last night and this morning to get some remote communication from her. But nothing."

I felt diminished. He continued. "I asked her if she understood what she was asking us to do by discontinuing her meds. "Connie," I said, "do you really want to die?" I asked her empathetically.

"She said, 'Of course I do not want to die, but I am in constant pain. I am almost totally confined to a bed. You have told me I will not get better, only worse, and I do not want to be a burden to my family or wither away in a nursing home. My husband is ill now and cannot take care of me.' She spoke so rapidly I could not get a word in," he said. "But she was clearly lucid, very clear," he said.

"She said that she wanted to pass before your father. She said she would not be able to survive another death in her family, and now that your Dad is ill, she is frightened. She didn't want you to be burdened with her care or the decision to put her in a nursing home. She said you wouldn't put them in a home. Now that you have said good-bye to her and made peace with it, she asked me if she didn't have the right to choose how to end her life. 'Isn't this quite enough?' she asked. 'Yes, Connie,' I answered. 'You have the right to choose.' With that confirmation, she smiled at me and closed her eyes peacefully. I'm not even sure what to make of this. The way she just smiled and closed her eyes—I have never seen that in all my years as a physician. She just closed her eyes."

"Well, she is not peaceful now. Look at her. You need to stop this thrashing. Do something," I screamed. "Stop all this now."

"You know I cannot do that," he said with his arm around my shoulder.

He understood my request. "I will call hospice and see if they can do something to make her more comfortable."

I just nodded. He patted my shoulder and began to walk away, but then stopped and turned back toward me.

"Oh, I forgot, one last thing. Your nephew, Philip's older son, arrived while I was in your mother's room last night. I hadn't seen him for a few years. He was very upset. I met his wife. She is very lovely, and quite pregnant."

"We had no idea," I said, my eyes wide with confusion.

As Dr. Spitzer faded from my sight, I stood glued to the floor. *Pregnant … wife … what?* I thought.

Early that afternoon, a nurse from hospice arrived. She entered the room with a whisper, almost tiptoeing. When she introduced herself, it was also in a hushed tone.

"Hello, I am Marilyn DuFrenes. Are you Mrs. Tullio's daughter?"

"Yes, I am. Why are you whispering?" I asked.

She replied, "When a person is in the last stages of their life, their senses are heightened; therefore, any noise becomes a distraction—it frightens them. The same is true for touch. You will notice how gently I am holding your mother's hand."

She was stroking Mom's hand very tenderly, and speaking in a whisper.

"Connie, dear, my name is Marilyn, and I am here to help you. Do not be scared. You will feel better soon."

Mom's eyes began to flutter. I thought she might wake, but she didn't. However, she definitely reacted to Marilyn's voice and touch, and her fingers moved within Marilyn's hand.

Marilyn looked at Mom's chart.

"They have her on morphine."

"Yes, I have been telling them that she may be allergic to it. I think that is why she is thrashing. Their answer was that they should give her more, eventually it will calm her. Instead, she is getting increasingly worse."

Marilyn shook her head in disgust. "How can they not see that she is having a reaction?"

I sighed, almost crying. "That's what I've been telling them all along."

"I will have her immediately taken off the morphine and we will replace it with Ativan and Dilaudid."

Marilyn produced a syringe of Ativan and administered the medication. Within minutes Mom's hands unclenched, her mouth slackened, and her head deflated against the pillow, until she finally lay silent, a solitary sigh rising from her lungs. The remainder of the day was quiet. I sat and held her hand, kissing her repeatedly.

"Mom, I love you. It's okay for you to go with Philip now. You need to go with Philip," I whispered.

I never thought I would be pleading with her to let go.

"You're right, Mom. It's your time to go. I will be fine, and I will take care of Daddy. Please take Philip's hand."

The day wore on. I fell asleep in the chair sometime around midnight, and on Saturday morning, January 31, 2004, I woke to a rapid breathing pattern emanating from my mother. She was beginning to skip breaths. I called the nurses' station with the call button. In a voice that held a touch of desperation, I asked the nurse, "Does this mean the end is near?"

"Not necessarily," she said. "She could go on like this for many more days."

My intuition told me otherwise, and it was always spot on. I decided to clean myself up in the bathroom. I brushed my teeth and hair and straightened my clothes. At 8 a.m. I made the decision to call the immediate family. Now I stood at the foot of her bed, too nervous to sit. Her breathing was shallow, ragged, and laborious. I had a bad feeling, and never took my eyes off her, listening intently for any indication at all. Then at 9:30 a.m., death came quietly, a veil passing over and lifting the rigidity from her face. Her breathing ceased. In quiet repose, her features were relaxed, eyelids lowered, mouth curved into a tiny smile. I was frozen in place. I couldn't even go to her as the swishing began again in my head. I felt that same catapulting that I had felt so many years before, and I started over the cliff feet first.

Within seconds they all walked in: my father, my husband and children, Philip's boys, Diane, Uncle Sam, and my Aunt Mary's son, Guy, with his wife. They all came separately from remote locations, but oddly enough arrived within minutes of each other. I arched my back forward and straightened my head. I had to keep it together for everyone else. This time, I didn't cry. My tears had long since dried. Diane was staring at me, and held my glance as something passed between us. I returned her gaze with my shock. I knew in my heart what had happened, and no words were needed.

I swallowed, reliving the quandary. Mom had two choices, her two children. One dead, one alive. She could go with Philip, while giving up everything—her daughter, husband, grandchildren, her life. Or she could stay with me, which meant renouncing her devotion to her son and pressing forward with emptiness in her soul. I closed my eyes, feeling her pain. Such irony, in the name of love. For fifteen years, Philip had presented himself to Mom at specific times and at specific locations. Mom had felt his touch so many times, and when the time came, she took his warm, guiding hand. For me, there was no other explanation.

Chapter 15

Dad went on after Mom passed. He visited the grave several times a week. I never saw any raw emotion, but he spoke of Mom with every breath. He assumed the household chores, doing an adequate job, and even shoveled snow every winter until dialysis became his master. He continued to deal with the everyday struggles of life on a machine, and the weakness it caused.

The air was chilled. Warm air whispered from my mouth into the iciness around me. My steps picked up as I reached the door and entered Dad's house.

"Dad, I'm back," I called out.

Quiet.

Again, "Dad?"

Where could he be? I thought. *I've only been gone fifteen minutes. He can't have gone far.*

"Dad?"

I felt my face flush, and I swallowed hard. Dad was not in the house. *Basement*, I thought. *Oh God, not the basement.* I walked toward the door and opened it. There he was, at the bottom of the stairs. I ran down, almost falling over myself. The steps were narrow, steep, and very old. At the bottom was concrete. Dad was in a partial sitting position, and he was conscious.

"Thank God," I said.

I extended my arm.

"Here, let's get you up the stairs, Dad."

I was able to hoist him up the stairs by his buttocks. When we reached the top, I pulled a chair from the kitchen table, lifted him, and sat him in it. Almost immediately, he began to vomit. As Dad teetered on the brink of unconsciousness, he heard my voice.

"Dad, Dad."

Then everything went black.

Tears brimmed in my eyes as I drove to the city hospital. I bore down on the accelerator trying to keep pace with the ambulance. When I arrived, the scene was all too familiar—fluorescent lights casting a glare in the emergency room, people fidgeting in their seats, tapping their feet. At the sight of me the nurse immediately showed me to the "special family waiting room." Waiting is always the worst part of a crisis, and at this point in my life, I had done it far too often. After waiting for some thirty minutes, I exited the room and headed for the intake desk.

"Yes?" the nurse asked.

"Yes, do you have any information on Frank Tullio? I am his daughter, and I have been waiting in the family waiting area for thirty minutes."

"Let me see what I can find out for you," she replied kindly.

As I began walking back toward the special room, a very pregnant doctor was heading toward me.

"Are you Mr. Tullio's daughter?"

"Yes, I am."

"He's not conscious," she says. "We are transporting him to Boston City Hospital, which is better equipped to handle him. He has had a severe brain trauma, and we've intubated him. If we don't transfer him immediately, he will die here."

"Not again. This damn hospital. First my grandmother, then my brother, my mother, now my father. This hospital is cursed!"

"Excuse me," she said.

"You know my grandmother walked into this hospital one day and never walked out."

The doctor shrugged her shoulders.

"I'm sorry. Come with me. We will give you all the paperwork you will need for your father's registration at the hospital. They will be quite busy with him in the trauma unit. You may not see a doctor for some time. They are a critical care hospital, and he needs critical care. I'm sure he will make it. I'm surprised he has made it this far at his advanced age. It's amazing."

"He has a strong will," I replied.

The doctor smiled a tender smile and touched my shoulder. She was the most compassionate doctor I had ever met.

"Thank you so much. You have been very kind," I said, and I shook her hand.

By this time it was late evening. I phoned Mark on my cell phone and gave him the news, and I began my drive alone once again. Thankfully, the roads had cleared, as I drove to Boston fearful of what I would encounter when I arrived. Boston City Hospital is in a crime-ridden section of the city. I was very apprehensive about arriving alone late at night and parking in an underground garage, but the flickering moon lit a path for me between the garage and the building. I looked up into the sky. As I approached the entrance to the hospital, I heard ambulances rumbling, doors opening and closing shut, and the clatter of stretchers as they were being wheeled in. After I registered at the reception desk, I was escorted to the waiting room, where I remained without word for four hours. The waiting room at this hospital was particularly depressing. Dirty navy cloth chairs, a coordinated dirty blue carpet, no TVs, no windows, no magazines, just me and my thoughts. I lined two chairs up back to back and tried to shut my eyes. At 3 a.m., a nurse came in to update me and take me to Dad's room.

I reeled from the sight before me and had to steady myself to keep upright. Dad was lying in a bed with needles in his arms and a tube down his throat. He was hooked up to several machines broadcasting vital signs of all sorts. His eyes were closed, and he was as pale and gaunt.

"The doctors will be in momentarily," the nurse said.

"Thank you."

I stood close and stroked Dad's warm forehead. I kissed him and shook my head. If he had only listened, I thought, but Dad was the most stubborn person I knew. No one knew that better than the woman who lived with him for almost sixty years. How had she tolerated it?

A moment later two doctors pulled back the privacy curtain.

"Hello. I'm Doctor Sanchez." He extended his hand. "And this is Dr. Morton."

"Hello," I said.

"Please sit down," Dr. Sanchez said. "First, can you tell us exactly how your father ended up here?"

"Yes. Well, I had just returned home with Dad from his weekly dialysis. He was hungry, so I said I would go down the street to Boston Chicken and grab him a dinner to go. He seemed a little shaky, so I told him to stay in the chair until I returned. I couldn't have been gone more than fifteen minutes. When I returned, he wasn't in the chair. I went from room to room calling his name. I knew he had to be somewhere in the house, so I opened the door to the basement and saw him at the bottom of the stairs, on the concrete. I ran down the stairs. He was conscious at this time, but unable to walk up the stairs, so I lifted him enough to get him near the stairs, and then he crawled up with me, hoisting him from behind. I thought he would be fine and sat him in a chair. Then he began to vomit. At this point I still thought it was a mild concussion, and I wasn't overly alarmed. But then I went to get him some clean clothes, and when I returned he was blacking out." I twisted my wedding band, readjusted my posture in the chair, and continued, "At this point I realized something was terribly wrong, so I ran to the telephone and dialed 911. When I returned his head was bobbing forward, and his eyes were closing."

"I see," said Dr. Morton. "Well let me bring you up to date on his condition. He has suffered a severe subdural hematoma. He is hemorrhaging in his brain."

My eyes widened, and for a moment I saw only white.

"He can no longer breathe on his own, so the machine is doing it for him."

"Oh, I am very familiar with that machine. It doesn't necessarily keep someone alive, does it?"

"No, not always," Dr. Sanchez said.

"Dr. Sanchez and I have deliberated and concluded that your father's prognosis is dire," Dr. Morton continued. "What I am saying is that we would comply with your wishes to disconnect his life support."

My eyes bulged and my breathing labored.

"Why on earth would I ever entertain the thought of disconnecting his life support?"

Dr. Morton stood and walked over to the bed. He glanced briefly at Dad. "If your father wakes, which is doubtful, he will not be the person you remembered. This we are certain."

"What do you mean?" I asked.

"We don't know exactly, but at his age the damage is irreversible. He may not be able to do anything on his own, and he may not even know who you are."

"You are saying may. May can also mean maybe not."

"Then I should say will," he said.

My stomach twisted into an enormous knot, my hands began to tremble, and now my lips were quivering.

"Take my card, and if you have any questions, they will page me," he said as he handed me the card.

"Thank you," I whispered.

As they walked slowly toward the door, I just sat in disbelief. Time flowed without my knowledge, until the door opened quietly again. This time it was a familiar face.

"God," I said, then stood up and ran to my husband.

Mark held me and just stared at Dad. His eyes were so wide in disbelief, they almost seemed dilated.

"God, not again," Mark said with tears brimming in his eyes. It's only been four weeks since your mother."

"I know, I know," I cried.

We walked over to Dad's bed and just stood and stared. I watched the machines as they monitored his vital functions and wondered if he was dreaming or just suspended in a void. Words were lost to us. Then, behind the chair, the door opened, and a nurse appeared. As she approached,

I continued to shake my head. She placed a hand on my shoulder.

"I know this must be very difficult for you," she said.

"You have no idea. I just lost my mother," I replied.

"Oh, I'm very sorry. We didn't know that. I can tell you that Dr. Sanchez and Dr. Morton are some of the best physicians around. Dr. Sanchez is a neurosurgeon, and Dr. Morton is a neurologist. They are highly respected."

I wasn't consoled. I wanted someone to tell me that they were wrong.

"Couldn't they be wrong?" I asked.

"Highly unlikely," she said.

I stood up and began to pace with my arms crossed over my chest, and for two more hours I paced, until I exhausted myself. Now, twelve hours had passed since the fall, and I could barely stand.

"Let's go home for a short time. I can't think in here. Can you?" Mark asked.

"I can't leave him like this."

"Leave your contact information with us," the nurse said. "If there is any change, we will call you immediately."

"Any change, no matter how insignificant it may seem?" I said.

"Yes," she answered.

Everything was surreal as we walked to our cars. Unfortunately, we had two, and the thought of a solitary drive home felt repugnant. Thank God the roads weren't busy with cars, because I swerved from lane to lane not caring enough to stay within the lines. When I finally arrived home, Mark was already there in the kitchen. With a glass of water shaking slightly in his hand he said, "You know your Dad's a fighter. He's never given up on anything in his life. I know he wants to live, and I think we have to give him the chance. It's only been twelve hours. The doctors could be wrong."

"Really?" I whimpered.

"Really," he said.

"Maybe I'll call my cousin Guy later this morning and see what he thinks."

I tossed my shoes and threw myself fully clothed on the bed. I didn't wake for several hours. When I finally did crack open an eye, the morning sun greeted me with a rainbow splayed across my bedroom wall. Was this lovely greeting a good omen? I certainly hoped so. I reached for my slippers and walked downstairs to the kitchen. I picked up the phone and dialed Guy, who was Dad's favorite nephew. Guy's mother, Mary, had passed away in 1986, and with Philip's passing in 1989, Guy had become much more attached to Mom and Dad. For my parents, especially Mom, Guy filled the void Philip left behind. For Guy, my mother became a surrogate for his own. Guy answered the phone on the first ring.

"Hello," he said.

"Guy, this is Donna."

"Hi Donna. How are you?"

I paused. "Not good. Dad had an accident yesterday."

I recounted the entire story.

Without hesitation he said, "I agree with Mark. Give him at least a few more days. He wants to live. He fights hard every day on that dialysis."

"I know he does, but maybe the fights over," I said.

"I don't think so. Just a couple of more days. I know my uncle."

"Okay. I hope you're both right."

"I hope so too," he said. "Keep me posted."

"Absolutely. Thanks." I took a deep breath and said good-bye.

Mark came into the kitchen and kissed my cheek. "How did the phone call go?"

"Fine. Guy agreed with you. I'm just so confused. No one should have to endure the loss of both parents in four weeks."

"You haven't lost both your parents. You can't let yourself think that way. You above anyone else should know your father better than anyone. You're just like him, a stubborn fighter."

I laughed. The laugh felt good. Mark nodded, then laid a hand on my shoulder.

"Let's get some breakfast, and then we'll go back up the hospital."

We spent most of the day at the hospital. Dad lay very still, the roaring of the machine the only sound in the room. I held his hand and talked to him the way I had to Philip.

"You're strong. I need you. You must fight."

I repeated these words over and over again, as I had so many years before, with history unfolding with such exactness. We slept that evening for the first time in several days. When the phone rang at 6:30 a.m., my head was buried under a pillow. Suffering from exhaustion, I tried to reach it, but Mark rolled over me and grabbed the receiver.

"Hello," Mark said.

"Hello. I am calling from Boston City Hospital with a message from Dr. Sanchez. Can I speak to Mr. Tullio's daughter please?"

"Yes, one minute."

"Hello," I said.

"Yes, this is Boston City Hospital. Your father has begun to breathe on his own. He is breathing over the ventilator. Dr. Sanchez would like for you to come to the hospital as soon as you can. When can you get here?"

"I'll be there in an hour."

I hung up the phone and looked at Mark with happy confusion.

"What did they say?"

"They said Dad is breathing on his own."

"That sounds good," he replied.

I let out a long sigh. "Yes, I hope so."

When we arrived at the hospital we immediately interfaced with a team of doctors and nurses. It had been three days since Dad had arrived in the emergency room. Dr. Morton stepped forward, smiled, and outstretched his hand.

"Your father's body has begun to breathe on its own. This is good; however, it is possible than when we withdraw the intubation tube, he could stop breathing again. If that happens, we would not reintubate. Do you understand?"

"Yes." My muscles tensed as I glanced at Mark. Dr. Morton continued.

"We will remove the tube today. He seems to be gesturing with his hand for us to remove it. You should be here when we remove it—just in case."

I nodded in affirmation. Mark stood by me and said, "He'll make it. I just know it."

A few hours later as we sat in the waiting room, Dad's intubation tube was removed. We waited and waited. Finally, I looked up and saw Dr. Morton approach. I could not read his face. I grabbed Mark's hand.

"Good news," he said. We removed the tube. He handled it very well. He has been breathing on his own for thirty minutes. His eyes are open and he is cognizant of his surroundings. We are amazed—actually, that may be an understatement. We will need to monitor him very closely in these next twenty-four hours. How much has been lost is something we won't know for some time, but we are shocked that he has come this far in such a short amount of time. He has had a severe brain trauma. You may go see him now."

There was a breath of relief, and I said, "Thank you."

As I walked quickly to Dad's room, I wondered if I should have said thank you. After all, if I had listened to them, I would have disconnected the ventilator before he was ready to breathe on his own. He would have died, and I never would have known what I had done.

Dad was lying in bed fidgeting to get comfortable. He rotated his head on the pillow when he heard us. A faint smile appeared. Mark and I stood next to the bed and just looked down at him in wonderment.

"The record books," I said to Dad with a grin.

Dad whispered, "I'm sorry I scared you."

"You remember?" I asked.

He nodded.

"You hit your head. Do you remember that?"

"I remember falling, and that's it," he said faintly.

Dad looked over at Mark. "What's that funny looking thing on your shirt?" he asked.

Mark was wearing a Harvard College T-shirt, and Dad was snickering at the logo.

He was back!

A nurse emerged from the hallway.

"He's still weak," she said. You may stay for a while, but do not encourage him to talk. He really needs to conserve his strength. He has been through quite an ordeal."

I motioned her to follow me toward the door.

"Yes, it was an ordeal, but as a nurse I must ask you, how could the doctors have been so wrong?"

She smiled and hesitated to give her answer. "Doctors are scientists. They don't always understand the human spirit, the individual will to live. There are miracles. I see them all the time."

"Hmm," I said.

We walked back into the room. Dad looked at us with a questioning smile. She checked Dad's vital signs and left the room. Dad reached over for me. He looked at the clock.

"It's 3:30 on what day?"

"Friday," I replied.

"Oh," he said.

I could see the wheels spinning as he tried to calculate how many days he had been unconscious in the hospital.

"Three days," he said.

I smiled. "Yes, that's right, Dad. Now you rest."

"Okay, one more thing, are the kids okay?"

"They're fine," I said, now crying full, round tears.

Dad opened his mouth wide, drawing in the deepest breaths he could manage. Each breath hurt a little less than the last.

Mark gestured toward a chair, and I sat next to Dad. I reached for his hand and held ours together on his pillow. His eyes fluttered, and he fell off to sleep.

Chapter 16

After a six-week rehabilitation program in a nursing home, Dad was released. I immediately set the parameters for his living alone. Things would have to change, starting with his car.

"You can't drive," I said. "They have suspended your driver's license."

"Really? Well, that doesn't mean I've forgotten how to drive, and the last time I looked, my beautiful white car was sitting in my beautiful driveway."

Mark spoke next. "Maybe we should get you one of those Life Alert things you wear around your neck. If you fall again or are feeling faint, you just press the button."

"No, don't want that either."

"Dad, you're so stubborn," I said.

He grunted.

"Okay, you're not winning this battle. I am putting a lock on the basement door. You will not be going down those unforgiving steps again. Do you hear?" I said, my voice rising several decibels.

"Fine," he said.

Well, one battle won, I thought.

"And we need to put some handicap rails and seats in the bathroom," I added.

"That's fine too," he said, "but you take away my car, you take away my life. Do you hear me?"

"Loud and clear," I said.

At this point I felt fortunate that the doctors had been so incredibly wrong, and I decided to pick and choose my battles. I looked around the house, peeked into my mother's empty bedroom, and then into my father's, where he sat reading the newspaper with a mischievous grin on his eighty-four-year-old face.

***

The guests had all arrived on time. The graduation of the Duxbury High School class of 2004 had been fabulous, the weather just the right mix of sun and heat. Dad sat on the sofa with his cane near his side. Since the accident just eight weeks before, he needed the cane for additional support. He had lost considerable weight and was still slightly pale, but as ever, his voice was strong, his mind sharp, and his smile wide. We couldn't ask for more.

"Sweetheart, congratulations," he said, as he kissed his youngest granddaughter, Kimberly. Kimmy and Dad were cribbage partners. Dad had taught her to play when she was ten years old. Watching them play, you could almost see the neurons processing in their brains as they tried to outwit each other. Kimmy was a smaller, younger, female version of her astute grandfather. "Thank you, Papa. And thank you for the money. As usual it is far too much. I'm just glad you're here."

"I know, honey. I almost wasn't, but you know your Papa. Remember, I was a sergeant in the army."

"Oh, I remember, Papa," she replied.

I smiled and thought to myself, *So he was, so he was. If only Mom were here too.* My eyes filled.

After the last guest departed, Mark sat down next to Dad. He put a hand on Dad's shoulder.

"How are you, Frank? Feeling okay?"

"Sure, I'm a little tired. Maybe we could leave soon."

"Anytime you want, Frank."

They sat quietly for a few moments. Dad appeared solemn and deep in thought. Then he shifted his body toward Mark and spoke.

"You know, Mark, Connie was a believer. She believed in religion, the afterlife, reincarnation, all that stuff. It was present in her life in a way that I didn't understand. It was central to her existence, but she never made it known to others. Her mother was like that as well, and I believe my son was too. You know I was never a churchgoer. I don't recall Orazio being a pious man either. On Christmas Eve, it was always the women who went off to midnight Mass. We men stayed home and played cards. We never really identified with the church as the woman had. We had lacked respect for the priesthood and were therefore detached. We couldn't understand the requirement for celibacy . Of course, the woman thought differently, and prayed. Connie prayed. She prayed and prayed, a lot, at night alone in her room, in that shrine to her son, with candlelight blazing around her."

Mark said nothing. For no apparent reason, Dad seemed to have a lot to say. Dad heaved a regretful sigh, remembering his wife and son.

"I suppose you could call me an atheist, or maybe just a realist," he continued. "I believe in science. I think it upset Connie that I doubted God's existence. She spent hours praying for Philip's recovery. Then after, she prayed for his soul, then her recovery. I think she was foolish to pray like this. If there is a God, he sure wasn't listening, or he was just plain cruel."

Dad's hands twisted in his lap. Mark remained silent.

Then Mark said, "I think I'll get your coat now and drive you home."

"Okay Mark, whatever you say, champ. You're the chauffeur," Dad replied.

Mark smiled, tears welling up in his eyes. How he loved this old man.

When Mark returned home and told me what Dad had said to him, I was amazed. Dad had never revealed so much of himself and his feelings. Never. In fact, we never really knew what he was thinking. I thought about it longer and realized I had never seen my father cry, not when Philip died, not when Mom died. How could that be?

**

Sited on a quiet hill above a busy interstate lies a cemetery. The landscape is lush and fragrant with lilac and honey-suckle. Sprays of water cascade down fountains adorned with cherubs. The water whispers to the tombstones, as the sun is beating down. It scorches the air and the marble, as it has for decades. In this cemetery, under a single tombstone, the past and the present collide.

As we approach, we help Dad, who is lumbering toward the gravestone. His gait is slow. He staggers artfully, his legs unsteady. But once he used to stride. With his back erect and his head held high, he marched through the streets of Belgium, France, England, and Holland. He spoke of his experiences often, especially in his old age. Pride exuded from his entire being when he would say, "I was a sergeant, you know," with a roaring voice that now sometimes cracked. Dad had denied death, and continued to defy life.

As we get out of the car, I reach for his arm.

"I can make it up. I'm fine. I've still got some time left in me. Stop fussing," he says.

"Fine. You just rest here against this stone, and Mark and I will start the planting."

"Look what I bought today," Mark says. "Miniature red rose bushes and red geraniums. Connie's favorite," he says proudly.

"Yes," I reply. "Mom insisted only red flowers be planted at the cemetery. She said red was the color of love."

I gaze at the headstone. Perhaps she believed that Philip could feel the sensation seeping through the compacted brown soil. We never asked her to explain her reasons for love. Mom was love incarnate. It emanated from her pores onto all that she touched. With my trusty trowel, I begin to separate the earth. Mark stoops low beside my knelt body cleaning debris from around the tombstone. Dad stands, supported by his cane, and watches. His eyes seem to be piercing the stone, almost splitting it. I notice the unusual gaze.

"Are you okay, Dad?" I ask.

With a distant look in his eyes, he hesitates for a few moments. Then he turns and stares at me for a moment longer. His mouth opens gradually, as if he is questioning what he is about to say. Again, he pauses and looks back at the stone, shaking his head a bit.

"You know through a man's life there are milestones, things he remembers right up to the very end. My mind is still sharp, and I remember it all. I remember your mother and your brother vividly." He catches a gag. "I hope they're together," he says. "They both believed in that stuff."

"You know one time, oh, a long time ago, right after Philip died, I came up here."

I think I know what he is about to say, but he has forgotten I know.

He continues, "I stood on this exact spot. It was freshly dug at the time, and I swore I heard banging below my feet. I am sure it was banging. It was almost as if someone were trying to bang their way out. I couldn't imagine what it was, and for a moment I wasn't sure where I was, but now I think I know. Maybe it was my heart pounding through my head. It was the thunder inside me," he mutters, still gazing at the stone. "What else could it have been? I heard it, and felt it," he says sternly.

He has clearly forgotten I also came to the cemetery and saw him digging the dirt around the tombstone. I swallow to steady my voice.

"I remember the banging, Dad. I still can't imagine what it was, but of course they're together. You must believe that."

He stands as still as an aging monument possibly can.

Soon we complete our planting. We gather our supplies, water the plants one last time for insurance, and proceed down the hill and toward the car, flanking Dad closely and in step. Mark reaches for Dad's arm as he helps him back into the car. The short walk seems to have tired him, and he winces as he sits again.

"Are you okay, Frank?" Mark asks.

"Great. I'm great," Dad answers.

As we exit the cemetery on this Memorial Day 2006, we pass five small limestone houses carrying the remains of generations of loved ones. These shrines with scrolled iron gates stand guard, in a row, at the entrance. I find myself holding my breath as we pass and thinking about the first time I entered this cemetery. Now as we leave, the sun is still warm, and its rays send a sweet fragrance up into the graveyard as the gate creaks behind us.

Chapter 17

I woke to birdsong and rose from the bed to look out the window. The sun was casting golden prisms through the morning haze. A warm June breeze grazed my shoulder as I began walking. Mark was already downstairs having breakfast. He usually drove up north to pick Dad up at about two o'clock. This morning, he had decided to pick him up an hour or so earlier.

Dad joined us for dinner every Sunday. It was his one day a week to be with his entire family. He would dress for the occasion with a suit jacket, dress shirt and pants, and sometimes a tie. Each week he would arrive with a different dinner wine that he had chosen himself for the occasion. He would hand the bottle to me, and say, "This looks like a good one, huh? It has a nice label."

"It'll be delicious," I would reply. It never was an expensive wine, but it suited the occasion, and Dad loved it, so we treated it like champagne.

"I'll call, just to give him a heads up," I said.

It was 10:30. I dialed the number and let it ring. It rang and rang, and finally the answering machine picked up. *Hmm*, I thought.

"He must be taking a morning nap, " I said to Mark. "You know sometimes he just doesn't hear the phone.

"Well, try again in a half hour or so," he said.

"Yeah. I will."

I cleared the breakfast dishes, made the beds, and dialed again one last time. It was 11:00. Still no answer. I felt a slight twinge of nervousness and decided to phone his tenants who lived upstairs.

"Helen, this is Donna. Is Dad's car in the driveway?"

"Let me go look," she said. She came back and said, "Yes, it is there."

"He's not answering his phone. I've called a few times. Could you just check to see if any of his doors are open? If not, could you knock until he wakes. I'm sure he's taking a nap."

"Sure," she said. "I'll call you back."

I wasn't overly alarmed. Dad always dozed off mid-morning and sometimes again mid-afternoon. After several more minutes, my telephone rang.

"Donna, I knocked at the door, but he didn't answer. I did see something I thought was odd. The Sunday newspaper is still on the front steps. Frank always picks it up first thing in the morning."

"Okay, Helen. Thanks. I'm going to send Mark up right now."

"I'm sure he's fine."

"Yes, I'm sure."

My stomach tightened slightly. Mark was alarmed when I told him.

"I'm leaving right now," he said.

"You're scaring me," I replied.

He jumped in the car and started moving even before I could jump in beside him. The tires screeched as he sped out of the driveway. As Mark drove north, he thought about his father-in-law lovingly. Marks own father had died suddenly of a heart attack when Mark was in college. Home for Christmas vacation, Mark had found his father gasping on the bathroom floor. He had tried everything to save him. He had shared more years with Dad than he had with his own father. He loved Dad, and he knew Dad loved him.

Dressing quickly, I continued my morning chores, with adrenaline pumping and perspiration settling in my body. Within thirty minutes the telephone rang. The noise was jarring, and I jumped a foot forward, grabbing the receiver quickly.

Mark parked the car along the curb. Breakfast smells were still wafting from a few of the tightly compacted homes. Nothing seemed unusual outside except for the newspaper on the stoop. He picked it up and opened the screen door. It squeaked as he tried the knob on the front door. It was locked, not surprisingly. Dad was compulsive about locking things—houses, cars, anything that could be broken into—even in this safe Italian-American neighborhood. Mark took the key from his pocket and opened the door directly into the living room. The house was silent. There was no sign of anyone in the living room or the adjoining bedroom, which was Dad's.

He called Dad's name. No reply. At this point his stomach was pitching. He moved swiftly toward the kitchen, and when he reached it, his breath was stolen. He saw something on the floor behind the bathroom door. He moved in closer. Dad was lying on the floor in the fetal position between the tub and the door. The shower was still wet, and his dress clothes were hanging on a hook behind the door. Mark fell upon him with cries. "Frank!" Mark felt a bone deep thudding, and touched Dad's forehead. It was cold. So was his chest, which lay bare on the tile floor. The skin on his face was waxy pale. He touched him and felt a shiver.

Despair settled over him like a mantle. What had happened? What should he do? Maybe it wasn't too late. He picked up the phone.

I put the receiver to my ear.

"He's cold, he's cold. He's on the floor. Oh God," Mark was screaming.

I started to spin, and I thought I was about to black out, but I caught myself and said, "Call 911. I'm coming!"

A second car screeched out of the driveway. On a Sunday at noon, the traffic on the highway is heavy, but I drove the breakdown lane whenever I could, using my horn and my lights, whatever I could to get me there quickly. As my car hit the street, I saw some neighbors still in bathrobes gathered in small groups on the street, some scurrying around and asking questions. I noticed the ambulance instantly in the middle of the road. I could not get my car down the street. I stopped my car and ran down the street. Mark was standing next to the ambulance as two paramedics were wheeling a gurney out of the house and into the ambulance. Mark didn't speak. The ambulance driver approached me.

"Ma'am, we are taking your father to the hospital. You can follow us if you'd like."

"No, I am driving in the ambulance."

"I'm sorry. We really don't allow that," he said.

Diane was standing next to Mark. I had called her on my cell as I was driving north. "Don't argue with her," she said to the paramedic. "She always wins."

"Fine," the driver acquiesced. "You can ride in the ambulance, but in the front only."

"Okay," I said, jumping in.

The curtain that separated the front from the back of the ambulance was slightly ajar. I glanced back occasionally and could see the back of Dad's head. Once I saw the paramedic place a large rubber bulb-like device over Dad's nose and compress it, but only for a minute. My veins were about to explode as we pulled up to the hospital. The ambulance driver escorted me out of the van before they took Dad out.

"What," I began to say with a confused look on my face.

"Just follow me," he said.

Into the family waiting room I went once again. I still hated that room, and I barely had the time to sit down when a doctor appeared through the door with a nurse. I knew before he opened his mouth.

"I'm sorry," he said. "He didn't make it. He had passed before he even reached us, possibly a few hours before."

My head went into my hands. "Oh God, no," I cried.

The door opened and in walked Mark.

"I wish it wasn't me who found him. Why did it have to be me?"

His chest felt scorched, as though a hot wind had blown through it—memories so intense he needed to steady himself.

"Dad would have wanted it to be you. Don't you see how much worse it would have been if I had found him?"

I touched his face. It was soaked with tears.

"I did everything they told me to do. I breathed into his mouth and pumped his chest, but I just couldn't get him to breathe back. I failed them both."

"Don't you ever think that! I know you did everything you could. It was just too late," I said as I held him close.

We asked to see Dad. I stood over him, my hand on his motionless chest. I stroked his hair and I kissed him. His flesh was cold and had the inert feel of the dead. There was a wound on the side of his head from the apparent fall in the bathroom. The years had chiseled deep lines into his once handsome face, and the dialysis had reduced him to a wither of a man. The lines beneath his mouth were lines of unspoken anger and unspoken passion. I closed my eyes and gently gripped his hand one last time. I stepped away from the gurney. Then I reached out for Marks hand, and he squeezed it. As I began to walk out of the room, the word "orphan" swirled around in my numbed mind, and the image of a sad, lonely child appeared before me.

That evening, as I lay exhausted in the bathtub, I listened to the thunder of the water rushing in. The longer I soaked, the worse I felt. My eyes were swollen from crying. All my emotions were overwhelming, and I felt as though I would drown. I stood up, toweled dry, and thought of Dad all alone in that house with no one around to help. I prayed it was a fast ending, as Philip's death had been. I thought about Philip again today. And Sarah. I haven't forgiven her. Like Dad, the tears in my heart formed concrete, cold and unyielding. I wish I could forgive. I wish I could do that for Mom, but I can't. It still hurts too much.

As Mark and I stood at the cemetery three days later, we remembered that only one week before, on Memorial Day, we stood here with Dad planting flowers for Mom and Phil. I thought about what Dad had said that afternoon. Did he sense the end coming? Was he opening his mind? It had only been two years since we had left Mom here. Now, standing there listening to Taps being played, I thought about how familiar this damn spot had become as I stood next to the casket holding the U.S. flag.

***

Kyle came down to breakfast the following morning, more enthusiastic than usual. At nine, he didn't feel or understand the loss as we did.

"What's for breakfast, Mom?"

"Anything you want, honey," I answered.

"Good. Mom?"

"Yes."

"I had a cool dream last night."

"Oh. What was it about?"

"Well, Nana, Papa, and Uncle Philip were on an escalator. They were going up, but I'm not sure where they were. I could only see Nana and Papa from the back, but I knew it was them. Uncle Philip was facing me. He was waving at me and said, 'Good-bye, Kyle.' Kinda weird, huh Mom?"

I broke down and ran up the stairs. I had lost them all.

***

It was very early. The sky had bled from lilac to pink, as I followed the coastal lowlands south toward Cape Cod. From certain points on the road, I could see the tranquil water of Popponesset Bay rippling ever so slightly. In the distance, I observed the house. From the outside, it looked unchanged. A very humble 1960s cottage, it had provided my family with many years of summer enjoyment. It was a welcome getaway from city life, and our refuge for over forty years.

The insides of the cottage could easily fit into the first floor of my house, yet it was comforting. It consisted of four rooms in eight hundred square feet of living space. The kitchen was warm and inviting, with buttery knotted pine cabinets. The pungent smell of the pine, like freshly split logs, spread into the room. I breathed it all in as a contented smile lit my face. The pine continued on the walls, almost encapsulating the room. On the living room wall, a testament to the ocean was displayed in all its splendor. A fisherman's net—rife with shells, barnacles, and various crustaceans—hugged the paneled surface. A screened porch spanned the length of the house, providing distant views of the bay. There were no conveniences, no clothes washer or dishwasher, not even a telephone. For eight weeks each year we would be cut off from our other life, and we liked it that way.

Across the street lay a small beach, actually a murky bay, where as children we would swim and dig for clams with Dad. Mom was the swimmer in the family, and Dad was the clam digger. The bay was never a sparkling sapphire, but more a steel gray, with small ripples that would quietly cut the surface whenever a small boat passed. Framing this placid seascape were many small homes, some with docks, and all with sun-bleached children sprawled on sun bleached decks. As a child as young as five, I would sit alone on the beach, a book in hand, looking out toward the horizon. I wonder what I could have been pondering all those years before.

Now, I paused with hesitation as I climbed the front steps. Slowly I unlocked the door and stepped in. The house was quiet and cold. The sensation sent a shiver to my bones. The house was not equipped with an adequate heating system, which I had remembered when I gathered my winter coat before leaving that morning. As I walked through the house and into the larger bedroom, my parents' room, silence drummed all around me. Odd, I had never noticed just how thick silence could be, just how empty this house could feel. I sighed a heavy sigh. For the moment I was quite alone, and the solitude clenched at my heart. Then I began to reminisce, evoking memories of late night card games with neighbors, the aroma of shellfish steaming in a large black pot, streaming through the open windows, Mom stirring the pot and creating something utterly fabulous. On weekends Dad would watch television with perfect vigilance as if he were missing the end of the world. Baseball and golf were his weekend television events, and on weekdays it was strictly news stations.

I swore I could hear the purring and lapping of the ocean hundreds of feet away. Images flowed like a soft wave as I settled on the edge of the bed. Here I sat, on my mother's side, the side closer to the bedroom that I shared with my brother. My eyes became heavy and fixated on the other side, my father's. The fixation seemed to propel me into a hypnotic trance. I could hardly move due to the stillness that gripped me. My throat felt dry and constricted, my tongue heavy. I tried to speak, but for a moment I could not. Suddenly, I began calling for my father, over and over again.

"Dad, please come back, please come back," I cried.

Like a tape recorder, I continued. Time passed, although I had no concept of how much. At first I saw no one, but then instantaneously the face and form of my father emerged. I told myself that my eyes were playing tricks on me, as the faint image began taking form, very slow and luminous before my eyes. The ethereal shape continued to unfold and solidify. My body felt heavy and removed, the grief and shock gripping me like a straightjacket.

"Dad," I cried. "You're back. You're back."

Dad lay still on his back. Dressed in what seemed to be a dark suit, his head was cocked in my direction, but it seemed almost glued down to the pillow. He smiled, his ebony eyes soft and virtuous, but he didn't speak. He nodded his head yes, then reached his hand out, his whole hand, inching toward mine. He grasped it, laid it on the pillow, and with his warm hand, he covered mine. I felt the blood rush back into my veins. Softly I cried, "I have missed you so much."

There was a noise. My eyes abruptly opened, and I flinched. My face was wet and squishy on my pillow. Tears were flowing down my face into my mouth. Next to me, my very warm hand lay on the pillow.

About the Author

Donna MacLeod's life has been characterized by many traumatic, mystical and wonderfully glorious events. These events have greatly enhanced the evolution of her spiritual character and views of life after death.

Personal tragedy inspired her to write this narrative non-fiction account of her family's struggle to survive the loss of her brother. In "Between Two Souls", she weaves a story of loss, love and afterlife spanning eighty-five years. She also demonstrates how the power of the mind can defy death or deny life, all without medical cause.

After graduating from college with a degree in Accounting, she was employed as a Flight Attendant, Corporate Trainer, and a substitute Elementary School Teacher. When she's not writing, she works as a Realtor, and spends time with her family.

"For as long back as I can remember, writing has been a passion. I simply needed a story to tell; one that would captivate. As life unfolded, with its myriad of experiences, so have the stories. I am telling this story to bring hope and peace to those who have lost loved ones, especially children, and for those who believe in the beyond".

Donna lives in Duxbury, Massachusetts with her husband and three grown children.